THE
LAW
ABOVE THE
LAW

JOHN WARWICK MONTGOMERY is considered by many to be the foremost living apologist for biblical Christianity. A renaissance scholar with a flair for controversy, he lives in France, England and the United States. His international activities have brought him into personal contact with some of the most exciting events of our time; not only was he in China in June 1989, but he was in Fiji during its 1987 bloodless revolution, was involved in assisting East Germans to escape during the time of the Berlin Wall, and was in Paris during the "days of May" 1968.

Dr. Montgomery is the author of more than sixty books in six languages. He holds eleven earned degrees, including a Master of Philosophy in Law from the University of Essex, England, an LL.M. and the earned higher doctorate in law (LL.D.) from Cardiff University, Wales, a Ph.D. from the University of Chicago, and a Doctorate of the University in Protestant Theology from the University of Strasbourg, France. He is an ordained Lutheran clergyman, an English barrister, a French *avocat* (Paris bar), and is admitted to practice as a lawyer before the Supreme Court of the United States. He obtained acquittals for the "Athens 3" missionaries on charges of proselytism at the Greek Court of Appeals in 1986, and has won four religious cases at the European Court of Human Rights.

Dr. Montgomery is Professor Emeritus of Law and Humanities, University of Bedfordshire, England, and Distinguished Research Professor of Philosophy, Concordia University Wisconsin, U.S.A. He is listed in *Who's Who in America*, *Who's Who in France*, *Who's Who in Europe*, and *Who's Who in the World*.

Dr. Montgomery has written and lectured extensively on the evidences for the truth of Christianity. A list of his related books and audio recordings will be found in the "Suggestions for Further Study" at the end of this book. These materials are available at www.1517legacy.com.

THE LAW ABOVE THE LAW

John Warwick Montgomery

*Why the law needs biblical
foundations / How legal
thought supports Christian truth*

Including Greenleaf's
Testimony of the Evangelists

NRP.

BOOKS

An imprint of 1517. The Legacy Project

Published by:
NRP Books, an imprint of 1517. The Legacy Project
PO Box 54032
Irvine, CA 92619-4032

Printed in the United States of America

Library of Congress Control Number: 2015938186

ISBN 978-1-945500-06-0

NRP Books is committed to packaging and promoting the
finest content for fueling a new Lutheran Reformation. We
promote the defense of the Christian faith, confessional
Lutheran theology, vocation and civil courage.

For

Robert L. Toms,

Member of the California Bar,

President of the Christian Legal Society

Preface

The recent grant of arms to my family by the Queen of England has considerably increased our interest in genealogy (a subject heretofore scorned when, as a librarian, I observed the queer people investigating *their* family histories). The first consequential Montgomery in recorded history was Count Roger de Montgomerie, companion in arms to William the Conqueror in the Norman invasion of 1066. Thus a better than average motivation led me to *The Norman Conquest and the Common Law* (1966) by George W. Keeton, professor of English Law and head of the Department of Laws at University College, London. There, in the concluding chapter, one reads the author's sober evaluation of today's legal climate vis-à-vis its scriptural backdrop:

> [F]or nearly a century Christian usages
> and Christian doctrine have been steadily
> legislated out of English law. As the late
> Richard O'Sullivan pointed out, the Com-
> mon Law had owed many of its noblest
> concepts to Christian theology. The soul
> of man was acknowledged to have an in-
> dividual relation with God, which tran-
> scended the claims of society, and, in con-
> sequence, jurisprudence was founded up-
> on moral principles directly derived from
> Christian theology. From this there
> emerged the concept of the equality of all
> men as bearers of rights and duties before
> the law, exactly as they were equal in
> the sight of God. . . .

If "Christian usages and Christian doctrine have been steadily legislated out of
English law," how much more so on this
side of the Atlantic, where today's temple
of the law has been fearfully weakened by
the rotten pillars of *Roe* v. *Wade* and Watergate? The only answer is to recover the
proper connection between positive law and
biblical revelation. With characteristic
forthrightness, Martin Luther, who had
himself studied law for a time, expressed
the perennial need for sound theology and
true jurisprudence (30 *WA* pt. 2 at 577):

> I know for certain that we theologians and
> jurists must stay, or all the rest will go

down with us. When the theologians disappear, God's Word disappears, and only
heathen, aye, nothing but devils, remain.
When the jurists disappear, then the law
disappears, and peace goes away with it,
and nothing but robbery, murder, crime,
and violence, aye, nothing but wild beasts
remain.

Two years later, in 1532, Luther was heard
to remark prophetically in the same vein
(3 *WA-T* No. 2832b): "Where there are no
people who have been made wise through
the Word and the laws, there bears, lions,
goats, and dogs hold public office and head
the economy."

The essays in this little book were prepared for different occasions (e.g., the
Christian Medical Society's Notre Dame
Symposium on Demonology; the Current
Religious Thought page of *Christianity Today*), but they all carry a single theme: that
law needs good theology and theology needs
the evidential perspective of the law. Even
the witch trials, by their doubtful example,
can teach us much as to how law and
theology ought properly to be related.

This author's viewpoint was shared over
a century ago by Harvard Law School professor Simon Greenleaf, whose classic essay, "The Testimony of the Evangelists Ex-

amined by the Rules of Evidence Administered in Courts of Justice," we have republished as an appendix (after carefully correcting the typographical errors of the earlier editions). From Greenleaf's *Treatise on the Law of Evidence*, the *London Law Magazine* wrote, "More light has shone from the New World than from all the lawyers who adorn the courts of Europe"; and his judgment on the reliability of the Gospel accounts stands as firm today as it did when he first delivered it.

If, as Lord Coke maintained in the preface to the sixth volume of his *King's Bench Reports,* Moses was the first law reporter, Scripture itself offers precedent for the argument of the present work. The reader might wish to consider these labors as a specialized commentary on the text: "Law was given through Moses; grace and truth came through Jesus Christ."

John Warwick Montgomery

Washington, D.C.
4 July 1975

Table of Contents

THE LAW ABOVE THE LAW

1

The Case for "Higher Law"

Cardozo's essay on "Law and Literature"[1] and Harvard jurisprudent Lon Fuller's imaginary cases in the mythical jurisdiction of Newgarth[2] offer adequate precedent for beginning with a fable.

Once upon a time a hare of philosophical temperament invited a politically orientated fox to dinner. During the entreé the hare presented an interesting argument on the relativity of all law and morals, stressing that each beast, in the final analysis, has a right to his own legal system. The fox did not find this argument entirely convincing on the intellectual level, but was much impressed with it practically. For dessert he ate the hare: lapin à la crème.

Moral: One's philosophical viewpoint can be of immense practical consequence, especially when the stakes (steaks?) are high.

The Need

First contact with the *Code of Professional Responsibility* of the American Bar Association[3] is a moving experience; here is a document reflecting genuine concern to hold high the ethical standards of a great profession. Closer perusal of the *Code*, however, elicits a sense of growing disquiet. Not that the standards are wrong; but what precisely do they *mean* at the points of fundamental ethical commitment? "A lawyer . . . should be temperate and dignified, and he should refrain from all illegal and morally reprehensible conduct." [4] To question such affirmations would seem, on one level, as sacrilegious as doubting motherhood or the flag; but is this not precisely their danger: they use the right words, but they do not define them; they continually beg the question of who, specifically, is to set the standards of "temperance" and "dignity," and who is to say

what conduct is indeed "morally reprehensible"? The practical consequences of
such vagueness are most serious; a recent
and penetrating analysis of "Law Schools
and Ethics" points out that the profession's
standards do not, for example, make plain
whether a lawyer *need not* or *must not*
"do for his client that which the lawyer
thinks is unfair, unconscionable, or over-
reaching, even if lawful." [5]

Throughout the *Code* emphasis is placed
upon conduct which shall deserve the approval of peers. "[I]n the last analysis
it is the desire for the respect and confidence of the members of his profession
and of the society which he serves that
should provide to a lawyer the incentive
for the highest possible degree of ethical.
conduct. The possible loss of that respect
and confidence is the ultimate sanction." [6]
Here the dubious assumption is made that
society will somehow maintain that undefined high standard of which the *Code*
speaks. The realistic possibility is never
faced that standards—even the standards
of an entire society—can decline or disappear. Interestingly enough, the *Uniform
Commercial Code* (hardly a document replete with philosophical insights) displays

uncomfortable awareness of this grim possibility; in the official comment relating to course of dealing and usage of trade we read: "[T]he anciently established policing of usage by the courts is continued to the extent necessary to cope with the situation arising if an unconscionable or dishonest practice should become standard." [7] The Watergate tragedy is an appalling example of the ease with which societal standards can in fact deteriorate —and it is noteworthy that this occurred in an Administration relying more than any previous one on the services of lawyers and the legally trained.

How precisely correct was the judgment of the Supreme Court in a case of personal influence upon public officials exactly one hundred years before Watergate:

> The foundation of a republic is the virtue of its citizens. They are at once sovereigns and subjects. As the foundation is undermined, the structure is weakened. When it is destroyed, the fabric must fall. Such is the voice of universal history. 1 Montesq. Spirit of Laws, 17. . . .
>
> If the instances [of selling influence to procure privately advantageous legislation] were numerous, open, and tolerated, they would be regarded as measuring the decay of the public morals and

the degeneracy of the times. No prophetic spirit would be needed to foretell the consequences near at hand.[8]

When public morals decay and the times degenerate, of what consequence is society's approval or reputation for ethical action? If all Cretans are liars, is it a compliment to be praised by a Cretan? And in such a situation, what is the individual or collective conscience necessarily worth? Conscience is environmentally conditioned, and the morals of the time will influence what is regarded as conscionable or unconscionable. Among cannibals, one feels guilty for not cleaning his plate.

The problem of establishing sound ethical standards in the legal profession and the wider problem of which this is but one aspect—that of finding ethical norms for the evaluation of positive law in general—becomes immensely more acute when we see total societies operating with legal and ethical values directly opposed to our own. Solzhenitsyn, in *The Gulag Archipelago*, eloquently and passionately condemns the dehumanization of the individual in the juridical "sewage disposal system" of today's Russia,[9] and his argument has been documented ad nauseam by others[10]; yet none of this impresses the Marxist-Leninist jurisprudent, who simply quotes Lenin's fundamental rule of socialist legal philosophy: "We have no more private law, for with us all has become public law." [11] In the temporary "dictatorship of the proletariat" prior to the onset of the idyllic classless (communist) society, the law exists pragmatically as an instrument of socialist policy[12]; and following Lenin's ethic that the end justifies the means,[13] the disregard of due process and the consequent miseries of political defendants and prisoners under the Soviet legal system are straightforwardly justified as furthering state interests.

Or consider National Socialist legal operations in the Germany of the 1930s and 1940s. After observing the situation in Nazi Germany at firsthand, Dr. William Burdick of the University of Kansas Law Faculty wrote in 1939:

> It is a necessary part of the machinery of dictatorships that the law and the courts shall be subservient to the ruler. In 1933, it was officially declared in Germany that the final authority as to the principles of the State and the law is the National Socialistic German Workers' Party; that no other political party could be

formed; and that the Fuehrer should make its laws. Does this declaration differ in principle from the decree of Soviet Russia stating that the "Socialist Conscience" shall be the final arbiter? Today, in Germany all judges are not only appointed by the present government but they are also subject to dismissal by arbitrary power. As a result, all Hebrew judges, of which there was a considerable number, many of them being Germany's ablest jurists, have been dismissed from all the courts. Moreover, this "purge" has not been limited to the judicial profession, it has been extended to the lawyers also. In 1933, the former German Bar Association was dissolved, and a National Socialist Lawyers Society was established in its place. All its members must be of German blood, and by official decree a person is not considered to be of German blood if his parents or grand-parents have Jewish blood in their veins. It was further decreed that all public officials of non-Aryan descent should be retired. This included judges, lawyers, counsellors in administrative law, consultants on cases in the labor courts, court officials, and candidates in training for the judicial or legal professions. In 1933, twenty-seven percent of all the lawyers in Berlin were of Jewish blood. Their citizenship has been taken away and with it their right to vote. No additional Jewish lawyers can be trained, because all Jews

> are now excluded from the German universities.[14]

As we are well aware, the sufferings of the legal profession in Germany were paralleled at every level of the society, and in the apocalyptic holocaust of the Third Reich six million Jews perished.

After the Nazi defeat the blood of these victims cried out for justice; war crimes trials were an inevitability. But what standard was to be used at Nuremberg to judge the accused leaders of the Nazi regime? When the Charter of the Tribunal, which had been drawn up by the victors, was used by the prosecution, the defendants very logically complained that they were being tried under *ex post facto* laws; and some authorities in the field of international law have severely criticized the allied judges on the same ground.[15] The most telling defense offered by the accused was that they had simply followed orders or made decisions within the framework of their own legal system, in complete consistency with it, and that they therefore could not rightly be condemned because they deviated from the alien value system of their conquerors. Faced with this argument, Robert H. Jackson, Chief Counsel for the United States at the trials, was compelled to appeal to permanent values, to moral standards transcending the life-styles of particular societies—in a word, to a "law beyond the law" of individual nations, whether victor or vanquished:

It is common to think of our own time as standing at the apex of civilization, from which the deficiencies of preceding ages may patronizingly be viewed in the light of what is assumed to be "progress." The reality is that in the long perspective of history the present century will not hold an admirable position, unless its second half is to redeem its first. These two-score years in this twentieth century will be recorded in the book of years as one of the most bloody in all annals. Two World Wars have left a legacy of dead which number more than all the armies engaged in any war that made ancient or medieval history. No half-century ever witnessed slaughter on such a scale, such cruelties and inhumanities, such wholesale deportations of peoples into slavery, such annihilations of minorities. The terror of Torquemada pales before the Nazi inquisition. These deeds are the overshadowing historical facts by which generations to come will remember this decade. If we cannot eliminate the causes and prevent the repetition of these barbaric events, it is not an irresponsible prophecy to say that this twentieth century may yet succeed in bringing the doom of civilization.

Goaded by these facts, we have moved to redress the blight on the record of our era. . . .

. . . At this stage of the proceedings, I shall rest upon the law of these crimes as laid down in the Charter. . . .

In interpreting the Charter, however, we should not overlook the unique and emergent character of this body as an International Military Tribunal. It is no part of the constitutional mechanism of internal justice of any of the Signatory nations. . . . As an International Military Tribunal, it rises above the provincial and transient and seeks guidance not only from International Law but also from the basic principles of jurisprudence which are assumptions of civilization. . . .[16]

Thus have the horrors of our recent history forced us to recognize the puerile inadequacy of tying ultimate legal standards to the mores of a particular society, even if that society is our own. To "redress the blight on the record of our era" demands nothing less than a recovery of those "basic principles of jurisprudence which are assumptions of civilization."

The Dilemma

But where are the basic principles of "higher law" to be found, and how are they to be identified and justified? Voilà the great dilemma: for however much our world cries out for absolute standards of rightness, they seem forever beyond our grasp. Like Ponce de León's *ciudad de oro*, the permanent legal norms for which we search appear always to lie on the other side of the next mountain.

And yet every day, in every court of the land, decisions are handed down in reliance on "larger," "higher" principles which do not themselves derive from precedent. H. L. A. Hart correctly observes that "because precedents can logically be subsumed under an indefinite number of general rules, the identification of *the* rule for which a precedent is an authority cannot be settled by an appeal to logic." [17] The same point is made in detail by A. W. B. Simpson, through analysis of the leading English tort liability case of *Fletcher* v. *Rylands*[18] (*held:* one is liable at his peril for the natural and probable consequences of the escape of any potentially dangerous thing which he has brought upon his land) and its qualification in *Nichols* v. *Marsland*[19] (*held*: defendant not liable, since an extraordinary rain caused his reservoir to overflow and flood plaintiff's land).

> [W]hen, for example, the case of *Nichols* v. *Marsland* was distinguished from *Rylands* v. *Fletcher* upon the ground that the escape was caused by an act of God, the court's acceptance of this distinction did involve some recognition of some justificatory principle of morality, justice, social policy or commonsense which was external to the law, and this will generally be found to be the case when law is made. For though the making of law may be justified by legal rules which permit the making of law by this or that person upon this or that occasion, the content of the law which is so made requires a different type of justification.[20]

But what is this "different type of justification"? We have just seen that the precedents of the case law do not necessarily yield it. As Bartley, C. J., argued in reversing a nisi prius decision based on a well-established rule of accord and satisfaction in the law of contracts: "When we consider the thousands of cases to be pointed out in the English and American books of reports, which have been overruled, doubted, or limited in their application, we can appreciate the remark of Chancellor Kent in his Commentaries, vol. 1, page 477, that 'Even a series of decisions are not always evidence of what the law is.' " [21] Professor Corbin of Yale, who includes this case in his standard text, *Cases on the Law of Contracts*, appends to Bartley's opinion this question for the student: "A precedent seems not to be conclusive. What is?" [22] What, indeed?

Equity lawyers have tended to locate the "higher law" within the sphere of chancery; yet legal history plainly shows that courts of equity, though they have often corrected the rigidities and injustices of the law courts, are subject to parallel arteriosclerosis.[23] The legislatively minded and the devotees of the continental Civil Law tradition see statute as the modern way to introduce justice into the fusty tradition created by anachronistic case law; but statutory injustice and stupidity are at least as manifest as the evils of bad precedent (one thinks of a Kansas statute that changed the meaning of π from 3.1416 to an even 3, and another that declared: "When two trains approach each other at a crossing, they shall both come to a full stop, and neither shall start up until the other has gone" [24]).

Other jurisprudents have attempted to penetrate behind case law, equity, and statute to some fundamental notion capable of supplying the needed permanent criterion of legal worth: Volansky, operating in the French tradition, suggests the jural concept of "good faith," [25] much in the spirit of our *Uniform Commercial Code*, which places central emphasis on this same concept.[26] Lord Radcliffe, in his 1960 Rosenthal Lectures, after admitting that "you cannot hope to get Natural Law in at the front door," tries to get it in at the back by way of the principle of "public interest" or "public policy." [27] Yet like the ABA *Code's* notions of "temperance," "dignity," and "the respect of society," these concepts remain vague and undefined—open to all possibilities of definition and redefinition by the society of the moment. What standard of justice would the concept of "good faith" offer in a Marxist-Leninist culture, where the end is held to justify the means? Would we be satisfied with the justice of "public policy" under National Socialism? In point of fact, such maximally generalized legal notions are like the chameleon:

they take their color from the societal pattern and are incapable of arresting degeneracy in the society at large or in the legal sphere in particular.

To compound the difficulty in the search for "higher law," some of the most influential jurisprudents and philosophers of our time have concluded that a solution to this problem is impossible in principle. H. L. A. Hart, after perceptively distinguishing between the "primary rules" of social obligation and the "secondary rules" by which a structure of positive law is created, identifies the ultimate secondary rule as the "rule of recognition"—the criterion by which law is recognized to be such in a society. When the question is raised as to the validity of a given society's rule of recognition (e.g., we might think of Nazi Germany's refusal to recognize Jews as persons deserving of legal rights), Hart answers:

> We only need the word "validity", and commonly only use it, to answer questions which arise *within* a system of rules where the status of a rule as a member of the system depends on its satisfying certain criteria provided by the rule of recognition. No such question can arise

as to the validity of the very rule of recognition which provides the criteria; it
can neither be valid nor invalid but is simply accepted as appropriate for use in this
way.[28]

Thus each society's ultimate legal foundations are uncriticizable, since any criticism
could only come from another society
whose rules of recognition have no more
absolute validity than those of the society
being criticized.

Hans Kelsen argues in a similar vein
that each legal system is a hierarchial
structure (*Stufenbau*), grounded in a basic
norm (*Grundnorm*). This basic norm gives
coherence to the plurality of legal principles
in the system and keeps it from disinte-
gration. But the question as to the ultimate
validity of the *Grundnorm* is unanswerable.

It is of the greatest importance to be
aware of the fact that there is not only
one moral or political system, but at different times and within different societies
several very different moral and political
systems are considered to be valid by the
men living under these normative systems. These systems actually came into
existence by custom, or by commands of
outstanding personalities like Moses, Jesus or Mohammed. If men believe that
these personalities are inspired by a tran-

scendental, supernatural—that is a divine
authority—the moral or political system
has a religious character. It is especially
in this case when the moral or political
system is supposed to be of divine origin
that the values constituted by it are considered to be absolute. If, however, the
fact is taken into consideration that there
are, there were and probably always will be
several different moral and political systems actually presupposed to be valid
within different societies, the values constituted by these systems can be considered to be only of a relative character;
then the judgment that a definite government or a difinite legal order is just can
be pronounced only with reference to one
of the several different political and moral
systems, and then the same behavior or
the same governmental activity or the
same legal order may with reference to
another moral or political system be considered as morally bad or as politically
unjust.[29]

The implications of such a viewpoint are
patently horrifying (Nuremberg trials are
ruled out in principle and the foxes of this
world can eat the hares as a regular diet),
but the logical problems in establishing absolute legal norms are equally formidable.
How exactly can a given society or a given
individual transcend the values of the cul-

ture so as to arrive at standards of absolute worth? In the 19th century Søren Kierkegaard, the father of modern existentialism, rightly castigated and ridiculed the pretentious philosophical idealism of Hegel; was it conceivable, he asked, that one man should be able to disengage himself from the human predicament—shed his own skin—to the point of seeing the World Spirit of Reason carry the human race dialectically to perfect freedom? Hegel had asserted that history would pass through four "world-historical" epochs, concluding with the "Germanic"; his perspective here turned out to be the product of the rising German nationalism of his time, not a judgment of universal validity.[30] But who—whether idealistic Hegelian, materialistic Marxist, or realistic jurisprudent—could see all of history so as to establish its total meaning, or survey and sift the universe of values so as to declare absolute legal and moral principle? As humorist and lay "philosopher" Woody Allen succinctly put it: "Can we actually 'know' the universe? My God, it's hard enough finding your way around in Chinatown."[31]

Contemporary analytical philosophers, though lacking in Woody Allen's pungency of expression, have made the same point with logical rigor. Wittgenstein, in his famed *Tractatus,* argued that our societal and personal limits as human beings forever keep us from producing absolute philosophies that are indeed absolute: "The sense of the world must lie outside the world. . . . And so it is impossible for there to be propositions of ethics. . . . Ethics is transcendental." [32] Metaphorically expanding on this theme in his posthumously published "Lecture on Ethics," Wittgenstein says: "[W]e cannot write a scientific book, the subject matter of which could be intrinsically sublime and above all other subject matters. I can only describe my feeling by the metaphor, that, if a man could write a book on Ethics which really was a book on Ethics, this book would, with an explosion, destroy all the other books in the world." [33]

To arrive at absolute legal standards, one would have to disengage himself from the world and its limited standards and go "outside the world" to a "transcendental" realm of values. Only there could the "intrinsically sublime" hornbook be found. To be sure, this is entirely in accord with common sense. Water does not rise above its own level; why should we think that absolute legal norms will arise from relativistic human situations? Archimedes said that if he were given a lever long enough and a fulcrum outside the world he could move it. Quite right; but all depends on a fulcrum *outside* the world. The very expressions "*Higher* law" and "law *beyond* the law" are suggestive of this, for they employ transcendental qualifiers.[34] The essential first step in the quest for absolute legal norms is the recognition that—however much we need them and want them—we will never find them by building jurisprudential towers of Babel.

Rousseau, who did not generally display such philosophical perception, formulated the dilemma with stark accuracy in his description of the work of the legislator:

> In order to discover the rules of society best suited to nations, a superior intelligence beholding all the passions of men without experiencing any of them would be needed. This intelligence would have to be wholly unrelated to our nature, while knowing it through and through; its happiness would have to be independent of us, and yet ready to occupy itself with ours; and lastly, it would have, in the march of time, to look forward to a distant glory, and, working in one century,

to be able to enjoy in the next. It would take gods to give men laws. . . .[35]

The Solution

The traditional answer to the cruel dilemma of desperately needing "higher law" yet not being humanly capable of creating it, is Natural Law theory. The essence of this theory, which held sway from classical Greek times to the French Revolution and which is experiencing a significant revival today,[36] is that absolute ethical standards and fundamental legal rightness are implanted in the human situation and can be discovered as the common elements in the moral codes and positive legislation of all men and cultures. Such Natural Law was formerly regarded as a product and evidence of God's hand in the world. In the words of Cicero: "I find that it has been the opinion of the wisest men that Law is not a product of human thought, nor is it any enactment of peoples, but something eternal which rules the whole universe by its wisdom in command and prohibition. Thus they have been accustomed to say that Law is the primal and ultimate mind of God. . . ."[37]

But what precisely is the "something eternal" in the laws of mankind, and how is it to be distinguished from the merely human, temporal, and ephemeral? This is a question of cardinal importance, for unless a clear distinction can be made it will obviously be impossible to criticize any given positive law on the basis of something more fundamental: what is considered "eternal" may turn out to be no more than "temporal" and thus subject to the same difficulties as what is being criticized.

Here is the crux problem in all Natural Law thinking. If the Natural Law is stated in typically classic terms—for example, in the formula of the Justinian Code, "Honeste vivere, neminem laedere, suum cuique tribuere" (live honestly, harm no one, give to each his own) [38]—it is, as Harvard's C. J. Friedrich observes, so "imprecise" that it does little more than to underscore the need for "some kind of equity." [39] When attempts have been made to specify the Natural Law in more concrete terms, the results have been either a listing of ethical and legal principles common to diverse cultures [40] (entailing the fallacious assumption, known as the "naturalistic fallacy," that what is universal is necessarily right) or an attribution of eternal value to positions, such as the Roman Catholic condemnation of "unnatural" methods of birth control, that are highly disputable.[41]

The most sophisticated of current Natural Law thinkers—those influenced by the analytical movement in philosophy—have been able to identify certain fundamental, trans-cultural ethical and legal demands imposed upon us by our humanity. L. H. Perkins argues, for example:

> The use of language implies a commitment as much as life in society does—a commitment to communicate, i.e., to use that language in a way that others may understand if they too are users of that language; i.e., to use that language properly. Thus, Jones has an obligation to follow through on that promise he made to Smith, and so does an anarchist who opposes the whole institution of promising—the obligation is built into the language, which is built into the institution, and the institution is built into nature by the fact that man is a political, i.e., an institutional, animal. . . .[42]

The reasoning here is impeccable, but it does not go beyond the most general obligations (truth-telling, keeping promises)—obligations of a heuristic or necessitarian character that are incapable of fleshing out the skeleton of Natural Law.[43] Specifically, what *kind* of contractual obligations should be enforced at law? Promises by cannibals, based on adequate consideration, to clean their plates? It should give pause that the vague expression of the *Digest*, "Give to each his own," was inscribed in German translation ("Jedem das seine") on the metal doors leading into Buchenwald.[44]

In the Preface to his classic, *The Revival of Natural Law Concepts*, Haines singles out this vagueness as the prime characteristic of Natural Law theories: "Carlyle, in speaking of the views of the Roman jurists on natural law, doubted whether any of the lawyers had very clear conceptions upon the matter. As a matter of fact all theories of natural law have a singular vagueness. . . ."[45] Is there any way of overcoming this fatal flaw? Considerable aid in solving the problem comes from the approach taken by the law-trained 1st century theologian in his confrontation with Stoic philosophers. The Stoics had provided the basic formulation of Roman Natural Law theory and it was from them that the great classical thinkers (Cicero,

Seneca, *et al.*) derived their views on the subject.[46] Thus it is most instructive to observe an early corrective to the vagueness of these views.

> [C]ertain Epicurean and Stoic philosophers encountered [Paul at Athens]. And some said, What will this babbler say? Others said, He seems to be setting forth strange gods—for he had been preaching Jesus and the resurrection to them. And they took him to the Areopagus, saying, May we know what this new doctrine is of which you are speaking? . . .
>
> Then Paul stood at the center of the Areopagus and said, You men of Athens, I note that in all things you are too superstitious. For as I passed by and beheld your devotions, I found an altar with this inscription: TO THE UNKNOWN GOD. Whom therefore you ignorantly worship I declare to you. . . . [T]he times of this ignorance God winked at, but now commands all men everywhere to repent, for he has appointed a day when he will judge the world in righteousness by the Man whom he has ordained, and he has given assurance of it to all in that he has raised him from the dead.[47]

It is the conviction of the Apostle that natural religion—man's search for ultimate values—is correct as far as it goes, but it does not go far enough. This search arrives at some notion of ultimacy, but its content is "unknown"—and would always have remained unknown if God in His mercy had not specifically revealed himself in the biblical history of salvation which culminates in the death and resurrection of Jesus Christ. "Whom therefore you ignorantly worship I declare to you." As applied to the issue of legal values, the vague generalities of Natural Law are made concrete and visible through a specific scriptural revelation of the divine will for man: ὁ νόμος διὰ Μωϋσέως ἐδόθη, ἡ χάρις καὶ ἡ ἀλήθεια διὰ Ἰησοῦς Χριστοῦ ἐγένετο. (The law was given through Moses; grace and truth came through Jesus Christ.) [48] Wittgenstein's "intrinsically sublime" book of ethics actually exists; Archimedes' fulcrum outside the world is a reality, so the world of human values can in fact be moved [49]; Rousseau's "superior intelligence" as legislator is not a mere ideal—and instead of being coldly "unrelated to our nature" and without "experience of the passions of men," God himself entered our midst, was "like us yet without sin," [50] and imparted to us the true nature and fulfillment of eternal law.

But why should such a stupendous claim

be accepted? And what about competing claims to divinely revealed law, such as that of the Moslems? [51] Admittedly (and students of the law ought to be the first to recognize it) to make a claim is hardly to prove a case; in the realm of ultimate values no less than in the sphere of legal issues competing claims must be arbitrated by factual evidence. It is precisely at this evidential point that the biblical revelation stands vindicated in comparison with all other such claims.[52] Doubtless this is why so many great legal scholars have been prominent apologists—defenders—of the biblical "higher law." Space forbids an analysis of their arguments here except for a brief mention of especially noteworthy examples[53]: Hugo Grotius, the "father of international law," whose *De veritate religionis Christianae* (On the Truth of the Christian Religion) (1627) stressed the reliability of the Gospel accounts of Jesus' life; Simon Greenleaf, Royall Professor of Law at Harvard and the greatest American authority on Common Law evidence in the 19th century, whose *Testimony of the Evangelists*[54] establishes the New Testament as documentary evidence acceptable to the courts—admissible and competent relative to its substantive claims concerning Jesus' person and work; J. N. D. Anderson, currently Professor of Oriental Laws and Director of the Institute of Advanced Legal Studies in the University of London, whose *Christianity: The Witness of History* and *The Evidence for the Resurrection*[55] demonstrate the facticity of Jesus' resurrection from the dead, and with it the truth of his claim to be no less than God incarnate and the soundness of his declarations that the Old Testament law derives from God himself and faithfully reflects the divine will.

When analyzed by the most rigorous standards of historical scholarship and by the most exacting canons of legal evidence, the accounts of Jesus in the New Testament are found to be the very opposite of hearsay; they are primary-source records produced by eyewitnesses.[56] "We have not followed cunningly devised myths," the writers consistently maintain, "when we made known to you the power and coming of our Lord Jesus Christ, but were eyewitnesses of his majesty."[57] If testimony is worth anything—and our entire legal operation is nothing without it—then the case for biblically revealed "higher law" is established not merely by the preponderance of evidence required in civil actions but to "a moral certainty, to the exclusion of all reasonable doubt." [58] The test was well stated by Shaw, C. J., in the classic case of *Commonwealth* v. *Webster:* "[T]he circumstances taken as a whole, and giving them their reasonable and just weight, and no more, should to a moral certainty exclude every other hypothesis." [59] How precise is the application of this test to the evidential case for "higher law" offered by the apostolic company: Jesus "through the Holy Spirit gave commandments to the apostles whom he had chosen—to whom also he showed himself alive after his passion by many infallible proofs. . . ." [60]

Benefits to the Prodigal Lawyer

If revelational "higher law" can indeed be established as a permanent arbiter of the positive law, two questions remain: first, what are its benefits? and, second, why has modern man—and the modern lawyer in particular—departed from it?

The benefits of an explicit, divine standard of justice ramify through all areas

of human life. We shall mention here four
of the principal advantages of the biblical
"higher law."

(1) *An explicit, non-question-begging
standard of absolute justice is provided, by
which the evil laws of sinful men and of
sinful societies can be evaluated and corrected.* No longer is one at the mercy of
the vague and undefined idealism of professional codes or Natural Law theories,
whose terminology ("honesty," "dignity,"
"temperance") can be twisted in virtually
any direction. No longer is one caught in
the vice of societal standards—which can
(and do) deteriorate under the pressures
of modern life. Why should Jews and Blacks
and members of other minority groups receive equal protection under the law? Why
was Nazi racism juridically damnable?
Not because of our current American social
values—since these have no more perma-
nence or absolute validity than those of other peoples—but because God almighty has
declared once and for all that He has "made
of one blood all nations of men to dwell
on all the face of the earth" and that "there
is neither Jew nor Greek, there is neither
bond nor free." [61] Thus is human equality
and legal standing regardless of race or

color established on the rock of "higher law," above the shifting sands of cultural change. Thomas Mann has magnificently captured the wonder and inestimable value of such revealed law:

> [A]ll the people came before Moses that he might give them what he had brought: the message of Jahwe from the mountain, the tables with the decalogue.
>
> "Take them, O blood of my father," he said, "and keep them holy in God's tent. But that which they say, that keep holy yourselves in doing and in leaving undone. For it is the brief and binding, the condensed will of God, the bed-rock of all good behaviour and breeding, and God wrote it in the stone with my little graving tool—the Alpha and Omega of human decency. . . ." [62]

(2) *Biblically revealed "higher law" offers the only reliable guide to personal and national health, and thus to the preservation of individual and corporate life.* The clear pattern throughout Scripture is that those who do God's will live and those who flaunt His commands perish. The "thousand-year Reich" that idolatrously arrogated divine functions to itself and ignored God's revealed law perished in a generation, "and great was the fall of it." Blessed is the nation whose God is the Lord,

and only those nations and individuals who seek first God's kingdom and righteousness will survive the pressures of a sinful world. "Higher law" is needed not only for sound legal decision, but for the very preservation of the legal system itself; flaunting God's law means the simultaneous collapse of society and of the positive law that cements it together. Again, hear Thomas Mann's Moses:

> "But cursed be the man who stands up and says: '[God's Commandments] are good no longer.' Cursed be he who teaches you: 'Up and be free of them, lie, steal, and slay, whore, dishonour father and mother and give them to the knife, and you shall praise my name because I proclaim freedom to you.' Cursed be he who sets up a calf and says: 'There is your God. To its honour do all this, and lead a new dance about it.' Your God will be very strong; on a golden chair will he sit and pass for the wisest because he knows the ways of the human heart are evil from youth upwards. But that will be all that he knows; and he who only knows that is as stupid as the night is black, and better it were for him had he never been born. For he knows not of the bond between God and man, which none can break, neither man nor God, for it is inviolate. Blood will flow in streams because of his black stu-

pidity, so that the red pales from the cheek of mankind, but there is no help, for the base must be cut down. And I will lift up My foot, saith and Lord, and tread him into the mire—to the bottom of the earth will I tread the blasphemer, an hundred and twelve fathoms deep, and man and beast shall make a bend around the spot where I trod him in, and the birds of the air high in their flight shall swerve that they fly not over it. And whosoever names his name shall spit towards the four quarters of the earth, and wipe his mouth and say 'God save us all!' that the earth may be again the earth—a vale of troubles, but not a sink of iniquity. Say Amen to that!"
And
all
the
people
said
Amen.[63]

(3) *Together with the revealed law, Scripture imparts gospel, thereby offering not only perfect standards but also merciful help for a fallen race that continually violates them.* Classical theology distinguishes three "uses" of the law set forth in the Bible[64]: the "political use" (law as the fundament of society, in the sense in which we have just been discussing it), the "didac-

tic use" (law as a guide for the spiritual growth of the believer), and the "pedagogical use" (the law as "schoolmaster to bring us to Christ, that we might be justified by faith" [65]). This "pedagogical use," which Luther regarded as primary, is the law's function to show us how far short we fall, as individuals and as nations, from the perfect standard of God's will. Perhaps we have not literally violated the commandments against adultery or murder, but Jesus tells us in the Sermon on the Mount that lust or hatred are the spiritual equivalents of such acts[66]; and "whoever shall keep the whole law, and yet offend in one point, is guilty of all." [67] Thus "all have sinned and come short of the glory of God." [68] But here the gospel of God's free grace in Christ enters the picture: He came to earth for us, took our guilt on himself, died to free us from the death we deserved, and offers restoration to all who come to Him in faith.[69] Luther drove this truth home in characteristically powerful words:

> [T]his is the proper and absolute use of the law: by lightning, by tempest, and by the sound of the trumpet (as on Mount Sinai) to terrify, and by thundering to beat down and rend in pieces that beast which

is called man's opinion of his own righteousness. Therefore said God by Jeremiah the prophet: "My Word is a hammer, breaking rocks." For as long as the opinion of his own righteousness abides in man, so long there abides also incomprehensible pride, presumption, security, hatred of God, contempt of his grace and mercy, ignorance of the promises and of Christ.[70]

Biblically revealed law thus destroys our self-image as just and righteous persons and forces us to rely on God's mercy in Christ. It gives us a true picture of ourselves, and teaches us not only justice but also mercy. Needless to say, these lessons are fundamental to the personal growth and maturity of men in general, and of members of the legal profession in particular. Without learning them, can the jurist ever pray, as all jurists should: "[N]ot a single time in rendering judgment have I forgotten that I am a poor human creature, a slave of error, that not a single time in sentencing a man has my conscience not been disturbed, trembling before an office which ultimately can belong to none but thee, O Lord" [71]?

(4) *In the face of the inadequacies and failures of even the best of human justice,*

biblical revelation assures us of a Last Judgment, where perfect justice shall be rendered. The entertaining volume *"Pie-Powder," Being Dust from the Law Courts,* written anonymously by J. A. Foote, K. C., contains the following anecdote:

> There stands in the market-place of one of our Wessex towns a memorial cross—not, indeed, ancient, and scarcely beautiful, but bearing an inscription which is still read at assize time with wonder and rustic awe. It tells how one Ruth Pierce, of Potterne, did in the year 1753 combine with three others to buy a sack of wheat, each contributing her share of the price. When the money was collected a deficiency appeared, and each woman protested that she had paid her full share, Ruth, in particular, declaring that if she spoke untruly she wished that God might strike her dead. Thereupon it is recorded that she instantly fell lifeless to the ground, and the money was found hidden in her right hand. The inscription adds that this signal judgment of the Almighty was commemorated by the direction of the Mayor and Aldermen for the instruction of posterity. . . .
>
> . . . So have I, when passing from the market cross of Devizes to the Assize Courts hard by, reflected how much more easily justice would be administered if all perjury were cut as short as that of ill-fated Ruth.[72]

But "ill-fated Ruth" is hardly a common phenomenon, however we explain it. "Justice is not only to be done; it is manifestly to be done"; yet, as a matter of fact, it is often not done, manifestly or otherwise. John Chipman Gray records the viewpoint, which has occurred to all of us at one time or another, that it is "an absurdity to say that the Law of a great nation means the opinions of half-a-dozen old gentlemen, some of them, conceivable, of very limited intelligence." [73] Our legal systems suffer from the fallibility of the sinful human situation: absurdities are made law; guilty men go free; innocent men are punished. But Holy Scripture promises a Last Assize, when "there is nothing covered that shall not be revealed, neither hid that shall not be known." [74] The Judge on that Day will be at the same time omniscient and just, and the ambiguities and failures of human justice through history will be rectified. Thus the biblically revealed conception of "higher law" offers eschatological hope: the promise that justice is not in the final analysis sound and fury, signifying nothing.[75] Scripture uses legal imagery to describe that Day, and stresses that the only hope for the individual or nation before the bar of eternal justice will be the services of the divine Advocate—Jesus Christ—whose death alone can free men from their sins.[76] His services are available free, through faith. Every attorney should therefore ponder, while he has the opportunity, the eternal implications of that well-known aphorism: "The accused who acts as his own lawyer has a fool for a client."

But, as a matter of fact, legal philosophy in modern times has very largely played the fool. In the terms of our introductory fable, it has created the conditions for its own destruction: the jurisprudential hare, by opting for moral relativity, has made himself a ready dish for the opportunist foxes of the contemporary world of Realpolitik.

And how did this sad state of affairs come about? It has been well said that in the 18th century the Bible was killed (by unwarranted destructive criticism, as in Paine's *Age of Reason*); in the 19th century God was killed (Nietzsche's "death of God" and the substitution of the *Uebermensch*, the Superman, who "transvalues all values"); and in our 20th century Man has been killed (in the most destructive wars in history). This degeneration is not accidental; each step logically follows from what has preceded: the loss of the Bible leads to the loss of God, for in the Bible God is most clearly revealed; the loss of God leaves Man at the naked mercy of his fellows, where might makes right.

A precisely parallel deterioration can be charted in the history of jurisprudence:

		In General	*In Jurisprudence*
18th cent.		Bible	Revealed Law
19th cent.	Destruction of:	God	Natural Law
20th cent.		Man	Positive Law

To the end of the Reformation period, jurisprudents grounded positive law and natural law in biblical revelation—where the clearest expression of God's revealed will for men could be found. During the 18th century, efforts were made by Deists and others to separate Natural Law from the Bible and to rely on "natural rights" alone as the basis of human society and positive law.[77] But by the 19th century a Natural Law independent of Scripture had become so vague that it was readily replaced by "legal realism," positivism, and other relativistic approaches. Then, in our time, came the inevitable holocaust: if law is indeed relative, it can be twisted in a totalitarian, revolutionary or anarchical manner according to the desires of those in power, and becomes no more than a tool of the party for effecting social change according to whatever definition of social value or dysvalue happens to be theirs.[78] George Orwell's *1984* appears on the horizon, as does the Antichrist of Scripture, significantly denominated ὁ ἄνομος –"The Lawless One." [79]

Like Western man in general, the modern jurisprudent made the fundamental error two centuries ago of thinking that human values could be sustained apart from God's revelation of himself in Holy Scripture. An attempt was made to live off the inherited moral capital of the Bible after dispensing with it. Eventually daddy's (Daddy's) money ran out, and the modern lawyer now finds himself in a far country "filling his belly with the husks that the swine did eat." [80] But—*Deo gratias!*—the lights in the Father's house are still burning, and a return to the "higher law" of Scripture is open to all. The prodigal lawyer need only "come to himself," arise and go to his Father, saying to him: "Father, I have sinned against heaven, and before thee." The promise is that he will be received with compassion: for this my jurisprudential son was dead, and is alive again; he was lost, and is found.

2

Witch Trial
Theory and Practice *

When confronted with the matchless claims of Christ—His life of perfect holiness, His atoning death to give fallen man the gift of heaven—unbelief finds itself hard put to sustain its negative posture. One of the counter-arguments most consistently employed by unbelievers since the dawn of modern secularism has centered on the witchcraft trials of the fifteenth through the seventeenth centuries: these horrors, it is argued, belie the claims of Christianity, for they were the direct and consistent product of its theology and religious practice; only with the rise of Enlightenment rationalism and the modern spirit did such abominations cease.

*This essay appears also in the book, *Demon Possession*, edited by Dr. Montgomery and published by New Reformation Publications.

Though the literature of the witch trials is enormous, as witnessed alone by the Andrew Dickson White collection at Cornell University or by Henry Charles Lea's three-volume *Materials Toward a History of Witchcraft*, the subject needs perpetual re-appraisal in the light of its function as a standard weapon in the armory of unbelief. Critics of Christianity by way of the witchcraft trials need to be reminded of the beam in their own secular eye; as Robert H. Jackson boldly stated in his closing address in the Nuremberg War Crimes Trial: "The terror of Torquemada pales before the Nazi inquisition." And Christian believers need to understand the true nature of the problem reflected in the witch prosecutions, so that when they repent they will repent intelligently, pouring no unnecessary oil on the smouldering fires of unbelief.

The Issue Sharpened

Critics of the witch trials almost invariably concentrate their salvos on the phenomenon of the demonic *per se*. They argue aprioristically that "no sensible person can accept the real existence of witches, much less demons," and consider it therefore self-evident that the whole concept of the witch trial was sheer madness.

It is not our task here to deal with the question of the ontological reality of the demonic, of demon possession, or of witchcraft—particularly since we have done so *in extenso* elsewhere.[1] To the convinced rationalist we would merely say: whatever you do, if you wish to deny the existence of personal, supernatural evil, do *not* examine the empirical data; for no facts in history are better established (except perhaps those relating to the incarnation of God in Christ)!

But wholly apart from the ontological question, the critics who pose such objections display a woeful lack of historical perspective. George Lyman Kittredge concluded his impeccable scholarly study of *Witchcraft in Old and New England* with these theses:

> To believe in witchcraft in the seventeenth century was no more discreditable to man's head or heart than it was to believe in spontaneous generation or to be ignorant of the germ theory of disease.
> The position of the seventeenth-century believers in witchcraft was logically and theologically stronger than that of

the few persons who rejected the current belief.

The impulse to put a witch to death comes from the instinct of self-preservation. It is no more cruel or otherwise blameworthy, in itself, than the impulse to put a murderer to death.[2]

These sentiments are entirely confirmed by the best of recent specialized studies. Thus, after examining the records of some seven hundred witch trials in the duchy of Lorraine, Etienne Delcambre concluded that the judges were anything but "monsters of hypocrisy and dishonesty": "Their language can reflect the highest spirituality—inspired, it would seem, by passages from *The Imitation of Christ*. . . . Their hearts were not hardened, nor was their love for their neighbor feigned." [3] In the same vein, Edmund Heward's careful biography of Sir Matthew Hale, Lord Chief Justice in the reign of Charles II, rehabilitates his activity in the Bury St. Edmunds witchcraft case of 1664 from Lord Campbell's incredible charge that he "murdered" old women. Argues Heward:

In his charges to the jury Hale stated that he had no doubt that there were such creatures as witches as the scriptures affirmed it. To a man such as Hale who believed in the supernatural and the revelations contained in the scriptures this would be irrefutable evidence.

All other nations had laws against witches. This would be regarded as weighty evidence by Hale as he set great store by the accumulated wisdom of mankind.

There had been an Act of Parliament on this subject only sixty years before, drawn up by the advice of eminent lawyers including Sir Edward Coke. How could a judge with Hale's education and background be expected to deny his religion, his experiences and a recent Act of Parliament? [4]

Except for isolated instances of judicial perversity (which are hardly limited to this single aspect of legal history—or of life in general!), those who participated in the witch trials ought not to be regarded as untouchables; they do not deserve to be faulted for holding beliefs inherent to the worldview of their day—and beliefs which (I would submit) have a disquieting veracity transcending the epochs of the trials. Proper criticism of the witch trials lies at a different point: the legal operation itself, as viewed in terms of *substantive* law (ought witchcraft to have had a legal remedy?) and *adjective* law (trial procedure

and the laws of evidence). Here, if anywhere, legitimate criticism of the trials
exists; and here, therefore, theological and
juridical lessons are to be learned. Let us
first examine the question of procedure in
the witch trials.

Torture and "Exceptional" Procedure in Continental Law

It is commonplace that torture was
used to extract confessions of witchcraft
and that rules of evidence were "relaxed"
in the witch trials. The accompanying judgment is also widespread that the responsibility for such an appalling state of affairs
lay squarely with Christianity, as represented by the medieval church and its Reformation off-shoots. But, as in the case
of most "obvious" truths, the truth lies elsewhere.

One must first of all distinguish between
two different systems of law operating in
the geographical areas associated with the
witch trials: the "civil" law tradition of the
European continent (operating in France,
Spain, the Holy Roman Empire of the German nation, etc.), and the "common" law
that became an identifiable legal system

in England after the Norman conquest and was transmitted to America by the English colonists. The continental civil law did finally come to approve of torture in a certain range of cases, including witchcraft; but this was due not to the church, but to the revival of absolutistic Roman law. In the Anglo-American common law tradition, torture was never condoned, except in rare instances where the common law was modified by statute.

On the continent judicial torture is virtually unheard of from the fall of Rome to the revival of Roman law. Where it occurred, it was roundly condemned by Christianity. At the time of the fall of the western Roman empire (5th century), Augustine had castigated the use of torture to extort confessions.[5] Influential popes of the early Middle Ages, such as Gregory the Great (6th century) and Nicholas I (9th century), reiterated his position and applied it to specific cases. The Saxon annals for the year 928 record that "good King Wenceslas," duke of Bohemia, destroyed gibbets and instruments of torture that some judges had employed. The twelfth century Decretum of Gratian unqualifiedly repudiates torture as a means of extorting confessions.[6] Concludes Lea: "This position was consistently maintained until the revival of the Roman law familiarized the minds of men with the procedures of the imperial jurisprudence." [7]

A. Esmein of the Paris Law Faculty is equally explicit in his great *History of Continental Criminal Procedure:*

> Torture is an institution of Roman origin. . . . It is, therefore, not surprising that the diffusion of torture coincides, in modern history, with the revival of the half-forgotten Roman law by the criminalists of the Bologna school. The transformation of the procedure by the substitution of torture for ordeals really begins to manifest itself from the end of the 1100s. . . . At the end of the 1300s torture had become a general custom.[8]

By the thirteenth century powerful efforts were being made by continental European monarchs to destroy the local autonomy which was the hallmark of feudalism and to create centralized "modern" states; in these efforts, Roman law—the law of an absolutistic empire in which the emperor had come to function as a demi-god—was an irresistible tool.

During the same time period, the medieval Roman church was endeavoring to increase its power through the parallel centralization of its administrative controls; Roman law here became the model for church law. Torture and inquisitional procedure thus entered the church itself. "The canon law had permitted it by virtue of the predominating influence of the Roman law" (Esmein, p. 91). On the European continent, therefore, the tragic irony came to pass that the church, which had endured the persecution of half-mad emperors during Rome's twilight, finally approved and practiced the same methods toward its deviants.

This gross inconsistency, however, was not lost on many influential Christian thinkers during the height of the witch mania. The endeavors of Protestanst Johann Weyer or Wier[9] and Reginald Scot [10] to substitute reason for torture are well known. Innumerable other efforts by concerned Christians have been buried in a general outcry against the trials; for example, few recall the painstaking and model investigations by seventeenth century Spanish inquisitor Alonso de Salazar y Frías, conducted with full regard for the civil rights of the accused,[11] or the eloquent arguments of French jurist Augustin Nicolas who asserted in his work, "Whether Torture Is a Sure Means of Verifying Secret Crimes" (1682): "I shall never accept as legitimate ground for conviction what has been admitted under torture, for it is an invention of the devil and has never been condoned by Scripture." [12]

Biblical Influence on Anglo-American Law

In England, the development of legal institutions followed a different pattern from that of the continent; in particular, Roman codifications had a much less pervasive influence. "Much of the common law of England was founded upon Mosaic law. The primitive Saxon Codes re-enacted certain precepts taken from the Holy Scriptures, and King Alfred in his Doom Book adopted the Ten Commandments and other selections from the Pentateuch, together with the Golden Rule in the negative form, as the foundation of the early laws of England." [13] The Common law of England thus did not allow secret tribunals and interrogation by torture. By the seventeenth century, observes Esmein (pp. 322-23):

Everywhere upon the continent, in France and elsewhere, the inquisitorial procedure, secret and written, was now established, a product of the Roman and the Canon law, with their defects more or less accentuated according to the country. One European nation, however, had resisted and escaped the contagion, and was destined later to serve, to a large extent, as a model for the legislation of the French Revolution. This was England.

Predictably, the loss of civil rights and the use of torture appear in England at times when the crown endeavors by any and all means to extend its royal power: the infamous Star Chamber of the Tudor and Stuart monarchs. But such a phenomenon was never seen as "normal" within the framework of English law, and the Star Chamber was abolished as contrary to the Magna Carta by the Long Parliament in 1641.[14] The most severe of the witchcraft statutes, that of 1541, was the product of one of the most absolutistic of English kings, Henry VIII, whose own spiritual life —it need hardly be added—was not above reproach.[15]

Far from being the center of the witch trial craze, as is often alleged, England and her Puritan colonies, influenced as they were by a biblically orientated legal system, maintained a remarkably balanced approach to the witchcraft issue. Kittredge has irrefutably rehabilitated both King James I (author of the influential *Daemonologie*) and the New England Puritans from the scurrilous attacks made against them by modern critics. As for King James, whose name is permanently associated with the Authorized Version of the Bible, his knowledge of Scripture was too profound to allow him the psychological luxury of witch hunting; after a detailed refutation of the charges leveled against him by Trevelyan and others, Kittredge writes (p. 328):

> Our scrutiny of King James' record is finished. No summing up is necessary. The defendant is acquitted by the facts. One final remark, however, may be made, in lieu of a peroration. Diligent search has so far brought to light less than forty executions for witchcraft throughout England in the reign of James I, or an average of about *two a year*. Contrast with this statement the fact that in ten years of the same reign (6-15 James I), at least thirty-two persons were pressed to death in the single County of Middlesex for refusing to plead in cases of felony (not witchcraft), or an average of over *three a year*, and that, in the same county for the same period, at least seven hundred persons

were hanged for felonies other than witch-craft, or an average of *seventy a year*. These figures call for no commentary. We may double or treble the number of witch-hangings, if we will, in order to allow for incompleteness in the published records, and it still remains true that the reign of James I was not, in this regard, a dark and bloody period.

A similarly careful study of Puritan witch trials leads Kittredge to the following theses:

The total number of persons executed for witchcraft in New England from the first settlement to the end of the century is inconsiderable. . . .

The public repentance and recantation of judge [Samuel Sewall] and jury in Massachusetts have no parallel in the history of witchcraft. . . .

The record of New England in the matter of witchcraft is highly creditable, when considered as a whole and from the comparative point of view.

It is easy to be wise after the fact,— especially when the fact is two hundred years old.[16]

The Desanctification Process

To be sure, in spite of Christian precept and its jurisprudential application in a not inconsiderable number of witch trials,

many instances of flagrant judicial in-
humanity did occur. In the continental civil
law, this came about through the application of the Roman theory of the *crimen
exceptum*—crime so heinous (e.g., treason)
as to allow the court to dispense with the
protections to which the accused was ordinarily entitled. Noting that "in 1468, witchcraft was expressly designated as *crimen
exceptum*," [17] Lea writes:

> In atrocious or "excepted" crimes, not
> only was the punishment severer, but the
> wholesome rules as to the character of the
> witnesses and of the evidence admitted
> were relaxed, showing that it was not
> simple justice but punishment that was
> sought. All doubts were resolved by resort
> to torture, both of the accused and of wit-
> nesses. It is true that careful and minute
> prescriptions were current as to what
> justified torture, but in discussing them
> the conclusion is reached that in the end
> everything is left to the discretion of the
> judge. It is the same with the severity,
> duration and repetition of torture. It is de-
> scribed as almost equivalent to death
> and worse than the amputation of both
> hands, but there was practically no limit
> to its severity except that if it killed the
> accused the judge was subject to investi-
> gation. Theoretically it was admitted that
> a confession extorted by illegal torture
> did not condemn the accused, but in prac-
> tice this was illusory, for to admit it con-
> demned the judge, and there was no one to

pronounce it illegal. There was one redeeming feature—the accused was entitled to a copy of the evidence and to competent time to answer it; but this could be
set aside by the will of the legislator. He
could also have an advocate, unless he had
an evil reputation or was caught *in flag-
ranti*, but the advocate was not to induce
him to suppress the truth. As to confrontation, when the accused under torture de-
nounced others, she was in their presence
to be lightly tortured again and repeat the
denunciation—the reason given for which
was that it was better sometimes that the
guilty should escape than that the innocent should be afflicted with dire torments. Such was in brief the system of
jurisprudence which developed the witch
madness.[18]

The use of such methods was bad enough
when carried out by secular authority; even
more reprehensible was their employment
by the church itself in the late medieval
period. Torture—categorically condemned
by the early church and its theologians, as
we have seen—came finally to be permitted
by Canon law as a result of the revival
of Roman law. Thus the infamous activities
of the exceptional tribunals of the Holy Inquisition.

Even common law countries were not
entirely exempt from such deviations

where witchcraft was concerned. Both England and New England accepted so-called "spectral evidence" in witch trial prosecutions. Observes Christina Hole: "Evidence that would have been unacceptable in any other case was freely admitted in witch trials. Michael Dalton in *The Country Justice*, published in 1618, says that magistrates must not always expect direct evidence against witches, 'seeing that all their works are the works of darkness, and no witnesses present with them to accuse them.' " [19] Significantly, specter testimony was done away with in New England as early as 1693—largely as a result of the arguments of Robert Pike, who effectively queried, "Is the devil a competent witness?" [20] More ominous was the theoretical possibility of torture in New England trials: the "Body of Liberties," the first code of the Massachusetts colonists, provided for the use of torture in eliciting evidence and as a means of punishment.[21]

How could such a sad state of affairs have come about? How could Christian believers—whose religious beliefs had been classed as treasonable and therefore a *crimen exceptum* in the days of Roman empire—have themselves jettisoned the legal safeguards of the accused in the witch trials? Two reasons can be identified, and there are important present-day lessons to be learned from each.

First, witchcraft was considered such a heinous crime and so difficult to detect and punish that "special" procedures were justified to stamp it out. The distinguished French jurist Jean Bodin, in his *De la démonomanie des sorciers*, reasoned that since witchcraft was so monstrous, "whatever punishment we can order against witches by roasting and cooking them over a slow fire is not really very much," and "one accused of sorcery must never be fully acquitted unless the calumny of his accuser is clearer than the sun, inasmuch as the proof of such crimes is so obscure and difficult that not one witch in a million would ever be accused or punished if regular legal procedure were observed." [22] This extraordinary admission makes patent that the evils of the witch trials were due in large part to the fatal moral error that the end can justify the means employed to attain it.

In our day we readily and properly identify this fallacy with the Marxist-

Leninist philosophy and with situation ethics; [23] but are we equally aware of its operations in today's anti-Communist witch hunting? Rolf Hochhuth's *The Deputy*—whether we agree or not with its theme that Pius XII was willing to tolerate even the racist horrors of the Third Reich rather than give up Germany as a "bulwark against Communism"—is a sober reminder of how easy it is even for Christian believers to sacrifice human rights in over-zealous crusades to rid the world of genuine evils.

Allowing the end to justify the means is but the surface of the iceberg, however; there was an even more basic moral failing involved when Christians allowed legal illegality in the witch trials. They forgot that God was still in His heaven and that His promise of a last judgment expressly applies to crimes unprovable in human tribunals: "There is nothing covered that shall not be revealed, neither hid that shall not be known" (Luke 12:2-3, and parallels). Faced with the near impossibility of making their case against witchcraft in the courts of this world, they perverted human justice instead of leaving the judgment to the Great Assize. They refused to let God be God. They *played* God and—inevitable product of such a game—dehumanized themselves.

The Question of Legal Remedy

Our examination of the adjective law of the witch trials (procedure and evidence) has thus brought us directly to a central question of substantive law: Should witchcraft have been subject to human legal sanctions at all?

Here the modern critic of Christianity gleefully cites Ex. 22:18 and related Old Testament verses: "Thou shalt not suffer a witch to live." But such passages, though they certainly have been used to rationalize witchcraft persecution, do not necessarily justify it at all. There are many verses in the Bible that pronounce in no uncertain terms a death penalty upon evil, but which do not at all imply that human courts should deliver or carry out that sentence. "The wages of sin is death," declares the Apostle in Rom. 3:23, but the implication is hardly that human tribunals should sentence all sinners to the gallows! And even if one concedes that the Israelites were expected to punish witchcraft with the death penalty, this in no way commits the children of the new covenant to such activity—unless at the same time one would bring the New Testament church under the bondage of Old Testament ceremonial law, dietary rulings, and slaughters of Amalekites, all of which served a special purpose in preparation for the coming of Messiah but which are abrogated after His incarnation (Acts 10, Gal. 2, Col. 2:16-18).

The proper function of human law is to regulate conduct so as to prevent injustice among men; it is not to regulate ideas or to coerce opinions. But, as Rossell Hope Robbins emphasizes in the introduction to his standard *Encyclopedia of Witchcraft and Demonology*: "Witchcraft was not primarily concerned with acts; it was concerned with opinions and ideas." No objection could be raised to prosecuting a witch for murder when adequate evidence was able to be marshalled to show that she had in fact killed someone, but the difficulty lay in showing a connection between her demonic *beliefs* and actual harm to others. Montesquieu, in his *Spirit of the Laws* (bk. XII, chap. v), gives classic expression to the issue:

> It is an important maxim, that we ought to be very circumspect in the prose-

cution of witchcraft and heresy. The accusation of these two crimes may be vastly injurious to liberty and productive of infinite oppression, if the legislator knows not how to set bounds to it. For as it does not directly point at a person's actions, but at his character, it grows dangerous in proportion to the ignorance of the people; and then a man is sure to be always in danger, because the most exceptionable conduct, the purest morals, and the constant practice of every duty in life, are not a sufficient security against the suspicion of his being guilty of the like crimes.

Some witchcraft ordinances made the salutary distinction between belief and practice; for example, "the Carolina of 1532 (based on the Bamberg Halsgerichtsordnung of 1507) punishes with death only injurious sorcery." [24] Sad to say, however, examples can be multiplied in the opposite direction. The learned Melchior Goldast, in his *Rechtliches Bedencken*,[25] cites the Schauenberg Policey-Ordnung of 1615 and other territorial Ordnungen to the effect that whoever makes a pact with the devil shall be burned alive even though he works no evil to anyone; "therefore those, whether Catholic or Protestant, are wholly wrong who teach that witches and sorcerers who give themselves to the devil and renounce God, but do no harm to man or beast, are not to be executed, but, like heretics, are to be received to repentance and absolution, with public church-discipline." [26] Thus the witch trials courts frequently obliterated the distinction between sin and crime and set themselves to the work of a miniature last judgment—but without benefit of divine omniscience.

It is vital, however, not to attribute this grave jurisdictional mistake solely to spiritual insensitivity or even perversity. Until very recent times, western man has not thought in terms of church-state separation in any serious way, and the assumption that state and church were fundamentally doing the same work lies at the root of much of the excesses of the witch trials. From Constantine's recognition of Christianity as the official religion of the empire in the early fourth century to the minority pleas of the Reformation Anabaptists for the separation of Church and State in sixteenth century—pleas that took another two centuries and more to be acted upon—the almost universal rule was "cujus regio, eius religio." The operation of this principle was especially powerful in the centuries when the witch trials were most frequent. To be sure, there was halting recognition theologically that something was wrong, as is evidenced by the insistence of the Holy Inquisition that those they found guilty must be turned over to the secular arm for actual punishment. But the great insight of Augustine in separating the City of God from the City of Man and Luther's fundamental distinction between Law and Gospel and the Two Kingdoms were not brought to bear on the issue of church-state relations or on the vital collateral question of the proper jurisdiction of human courts.

The blending of church and state is of course a spiritual problem in itself. Luther rightly emphasized that whenever Law and Gospel are confused—whenever a mélange of the Two Kingdoms occurs—human pride and works righteousness lie at the root. Man wants to carry out God's functions; he wants to build new towers of Babel to reach heaven. Not satisfied with the areas of civil and legal control given to him ("subdue the earth"—Gen. 1:28), man tries also to subdue hell. In the case of the witch trials, irony is piled upon irony, for in an effort to conquer the devil by whatever means, man falls directly into the clutches of the

evil one. It was the primal sin of Lucifer
to say, "I will be like the most High" (Isa.
14:12-15). Thus did the son of the morning
become the prince of darkness; and thus
were the Christians who played God in the
witch trials historically tainted with the
mark of the beast they endeavored to subdue in an unscriptural way.

Again, the witch trials hold out a warning for the contemporary church. We also—
with no excuse available by way of established religion, since the separation of
church and state is integral to our constitutional law—press for the expansion of legal
remedies in moral and spiritual realms.
Evangelicals have a long and sorry history
of pushing for the legal enforcement of
morals (local option campaigns, Sunday
closing laws, and the like). Where, as in
the case of literary censorship, the causal
connection between wrong belief and direct
injury is as hard to establish as it was in
the witchcraft trials, are we not doing the
Faith a great disservice to press for legal
sanctions? Ought we not to keep before
us the fundamental distinction between
God's tribunal and man's, between His
kingdom and ours, between eternal gospel
and temporal law? Our task is not to cor-

rect every moral failing by human legislation; we are rather to legislate where provable harm to the body politic will arise in the absence of law. Thus we must prosecute stealing, but not profanity; perjury and misrepresentation of the terms of a contract, but not lying in general; child abuse, but not the teaching of atheism; murder, but not belief in witchcraft. God is still in His heaven, and the evils we are powerless to correct in accord with His Word He will most assuredly remedy on the last day.

Some Witch Trial Lessons Summarized

History is a good schoolteacher. Here, in summary, are lessons which contemporary Christians can and should learn from the witch trials.

(1) Properly distinguish state from church, human courts from the last judgment, Law from Gospel.

(2) In correcting evils, never yield to the situationist principle of the end justifying the means.

(3) Be most careful not to assimilate the evil methods of your adversaries in

combatting them. As a result of taking the gold of the Egyptians, the Israelites had the wherewithal to make a golden calf; medieval Christians, having conquered ancient Rome, uncritically absorbed her law, thereby acquiring a positive view of judicial torture and "extra-ordinary" procedures inimical to civil rights and scriptural humanitarianism.

(4) Never underestimate your spiritual opposition. Even after all appropriate qualifications have been made, the devil achieved more through the witch trials than he could possibly have gained by demonic activity apart from them.

3

Legal Reasoning and
Christian Apologetics*

The interrelations of law and theology are multifarious, and one of the most striking lies at their point of conjunction in apologetic task.

Readers of older apologetic literature are aware that lawyers and legal scholars have often been concerned with the credibility of Christianity. The "founder of modern apologetics" by way of his classic work, *The Truth of the Christian Religion* (1627), was Hugo Grotius—and he is even more well known as the "father of international

---

*First published in *Christianity Today*, February 14, 1975, and here revised.

law" for his treatise on *The Law of War and Peace* (1625). The greatest authority on American common-law evidence in the 19th century was Harvard Law School professor Simon Greenleaf (his status was similar to Wigmore's in our own century), and he was the author of the still published *Testimony of the Evangelists,* a demonstration of the reliability of the Gospel accounts of our Lord's life. Irwin Linton's popular volume, *A Lawyer Examines the Bible,* the tracts and booklets of J. N. D. Anderson (director of the University of London's Institute of Advanced Legal Studies), and the writings of Jacques Ellul (professor of law at Bordeaux) are a valuable barometer of the extent to which the legal mind is drawn like a moth to the flame of apologetics.

Why does this occur? Why are lawyers more inclined to do apologetics than engineers or dentists? One reason might be that the law plays a very large role in Scripture itself—not only through the Old Testament covenant of law but also in the centrality of the trial of Jesus and Pauline legal imagery in the New Testament; thus such works as A. N. Sherwin-White's *Roman Society and Roman Law in the New Testament* (1963), with their powerful apologetic overtones. But an even more important reason lies in the very nature of the legal operation.

In spite of the popular notion that lawyers are sophists who (to use the language of Plato's *Apology of Socrates)* "make the worse argument appear the better," the fundamental function of the legal profession is to seek justice by seeking truth. The lawyer endeavors to reduce societal conflicts by arbitrating conflicting truth-claims. Inherent to the practice of the law is an effort to resolve conflicts over legal responsibility, and such conflicts invariably turn on questions of fact. To establish a "cause of action" the plaintiff's complaint must allege a legal right which the defendant was duty-bound to recognize, and which he violated; at the trial evidentiary facts must be marshalled in support of the plaintiff's allegations, and the defendant will need to provide factual evidence in his behalf to counter the plaintiff's prima facie case against him. To this end, legal science, as an outgrowth of millenia of court decisions, developed meticulous criteria for distinguishing factual truth from error. The preoccupation of the law with conons of evidence creates a natural interest on the part of lawyers to investigate religious truth-claims.

Concretely, here are some fundamental principles of the law of evidence, which, if applied to the question of the factual truth of Christianity, will yield most significant results: (1) The "ancient documents" rule: ancient documents will be received as competent evidence if they are "fair on their face" (i.e., offer no internal evidence of tampering) and have been maintained in "reasonable custody" (i.e., their preservation has been consistent with their content). Applied to the Gospel records, and reinforced by responsible lower (textual) criticism, this rule would establish their competency in any court of law.

(2) The "parol evidence" rule: external, oral testimony or tradition will not be received in evidence to add to, subtract from, vary, or contradict an executed written instrument such as a will. Applied to the biblical documents, which expressly claim to be "executed" and complete (Rev. 22:18-19), this rule insists that the Scripture be allowed to "interpret itself" and not be twisted by external, extra-biblical data (comparative New Eastern religious texts and practices, Sitz im Leben inter-

pretations, "historical-critical method," "New Hermeneutic," etc.).

(3) The "hearsay rule"—what Wigmore calls the "proudest scion of our jury-trial rules of evidence": a witness must testify "of his own knowledge," not on the basis of what has come to him indirectly from others. Applied to the New Testament documents, this demand for primary-source evidence is fully vindicated by the constant asseverations of their authors to be setting forth "that which we have heard, which we have seen with our eyes, which we have looked upon, and our hands have handled, the Word of life" (1 John 1:1).

(4) The related "cross-examination" principle: "All trials proceed upon the idea that some confidence is due to human testimony, and that this confidence grows and becomes more steadfast in proportion as the witness has been subjected to a close and searching cross-examination" (Justice Ruffin, in *State* v. *Morriss*, 84 N.C. 764). Applied to the apostolic proclamation, this rule underscores the reliability of testimony to Christ's resurrection which was presented contemporaneously in the synagogues—in the very teeth of opposition, among hostile cross-examiners who would

certainly have destroyed the case for Christianity had the facts been otherwise.

These apologetic applications of legal reasoning are a mere sampling. What makes them particularly important is the place of the legal system in society: the indisputable consideration that upon just such rules of evidence issues of life and death are necessarily decided and man's societal fate is determined. Analytical philosopher Stephen Toulmin, in his ground breaking work, *The Uses of Argument* (1958), goes so far as to recommend that philosophy itself ceases to rely primarily the deductive, mathematical, Cartesian model to solve its metaphysical problems, and instead "treat logic as generalised jurisprudence"—learn from the inductive, fact-orientated structure of legal argument. Such an approach would accord well with the twofold stress of modern Wittgensteinian thought on the necessity of verification and the importance of doing philosophy within the framework of ordinary language. Apologetically, the modern man faced with legally grounded evidence for Christ's claims is in the awkward position of having to go to the Cross or throw away the only accepted method of arbitrating ultimate questions in society. Luther put it nicely in the *Tischreden:* "If the world will not hear the divines, they must hear the lawyers, who will teach them manners."

APPENDIX A

The Testimony of the Evangelists

by Simon Greenleaf [1]

In examining the evidences of the Christian religion, it is essential to the discovery of truth that we bring to the investigation a mind freed, as far as possible, from existing prejudice, and open to conviction. There should be a readiness, on our part, to investigate with candor, to follow the truth wherever it may lead us, and to submit, without reserve or objection, to all the teachings of this religion, if it be found to be of divine origin. "There is no other entrance," says Lord Bacon, "to the kingdom of man, which is founded in the sciences, than to the kingdom of heaven, into which no one can enter but in the character of a little child." [2] The docility which true philosophy requires of her disciples is not a spirit of servility, or the surrender of the reason and judgment to whatsoever the teacher may inculcate; but it is a mind free from all pride of opinion, not hostile to the truth sought for, willing to pursue the inquiry, and impartially to weigh the arguments and evidence, and to acquiesce in the judgment of right reason. The investigation, moreover, should be pursued with the serious earnestness which becomes the greatness of the subject—a subject fraught with such momentous consequences to man. It should be pursued as in the presence of God, and under the solemn sanctions created by a lively sense of his omniscience, and of our accountability to him for the right use of the faculties which he has bestowed.

In requiring this candor and simplicity of mind in those who would investigate the truth of our religion, Christianity demands nothing more than is readily conceded to every branch of human science. All these have their data, and their axioms; and Christianity, too, has her first principles, the admission of which is essential to any real progress in knowledge. "Christianity," says Bishop Wilson, "inscribes on the portal of her dominion 'Whosoever shall not receive the kingdom of God as a little child, shall in nowise enter therein.' Christianity does not profess to convince the perverse and headstrong, to bring irresistible evidence to the daring and profane, to vanquish the proud scorner, and afford evidences from which the careless and perverse cannot possibly escape. This might go to destroy man's responsibility. All that Christianity professes, is to propose such evidences as may satisfy the meek, the tractable, the candid, the serious inquirer." [3]

The present design, however, is not to enter upon any general examination of the evidences of Christianity, but to confine the inquiry to the testimony of the Four Evangelists, bringing their narratives to the tests to which other evidence is subjected in human tribunals. The foundation of our religion is a basis of fact—the fact of the birth, ministry, miracles, death, resurrection, and ascension of Jesus Christ. These are related by the Evangelists as having actually occurred, within their own personal knowledge. Our religion, then, rests on the credit due to these witnesses. Are they worthy of implicit belief, in the matters which they relate? This is the question, in all human tribunals, in regard to persons testifying before them; and we propose to test the veracity of these witnesses, by the same rules and means which are there employed. The importance of the facts testified, and their relations to the affairs of the soul, and the life to come, can make no difference in the principles or the mode of weighing the evidence. It is still the evidence of matters of fact, capable of being seen and known and related, as well by one man as by another. And if the testimony of the Evangelist, supposing it to be relevant and material to the issue in a question of property or of personal right, between man and man, in a court of justice, ought to be believed and have weight; then, upon the like principles, it ought to receive our entire credit here. But if, on the other hand, we should be justified in rejecting it, if there testified on oath, then, supposing our rules of evidence to be sound, we may be excused if we hesitate elsewhere to give it credence.

The proof that God has revealed himself to man by special and express communications, and that Christianity constitutes that revelation, is no part of these inquiries. This has already been shown, in the most satisfactory manner, by others, who have written expressly upon this subject.[4] Referring therefore to their writings for the arguments and proofs, the fact will here

be assumed as true. That man is a religious being, is universally conceded, for it has been seen
to be universally true. He is everywhere a worshiper. In every age and country, and in every
stage, from the highest intellectual culture to
the darkest stupidity, he bows with homage to
a superior Being. Be it the rude-carved idol of
his own fabrication, or the unseen divinity that
stirs within him, it is still the object of his adora-
tion. This trait in the character of man is so
uniform, that it may safely be assumed, either
as one of the original attributes of his nature,
or as necessarily resulting from the action of
one or more of those attributes.

The object of man's worship, whatever it be,
will naturally be his standard of perfection. He
clothes it with every attribute, belonging, in his
view, to a perfect character; and this character
he himself endeavors to attain. He may not,
directly and consciously, aim to acquire every
virtue of his deity, and to avoid the opposite
vices; but still this will be the inevitable consequence of sincere and constant worship. As in
human society men become assimilated, both
in manners and moral principles, to their chosen
associates, so in the worship of whatever deity
men adore, they "form to him the relish of their
souls." To suppose, then, that God made man
capable of religion, and requiring it in order
to the development of the highest part of his
nature, without communicating with him, as a
father, in those revelations which alone could
perfect that nature, would be a reproach upon
God, and a contradiction.[5]

How it came to pass that man, originally
taught, as we doubt not he was, to know and
to worship the true Jehovah, is found, at so early

a period of his history, a worshiper of baser
objects, it is foreign to our present purpose to
inquire. But the fact is lamentably true, that
he soon became an idolator, a worshiper of moral abominations. The Scythians and Northmen
adored the impersonations of heroic valor and
of bloodthirsty and cruel revenge. The mythol-
ogy of Greece and of Rome, though it exhibited
a few examples of virtue and goodness, abound-
ed in others of gross licentiousness and vice.
The gods of Egypt were reptiles, and beasts
and birds. The religion of Central and Eastern
Asia was polluted with lust and cruelty, and
smeared with blood, rioting, in deadly triumph,
over all the tender affections of the human heart
and all the convictions of the human understanding. Western and Southern Africa and Poly-
nesia are, to this day, the abodes of frightful
idolatry, cannibalism, and cruelty; and the abor-
igines of both the Americas are examples of
the depths of superstition to which the human
mind may be debased. In every quarter of the
world, however, there is a striking uniformity
seen in all the features of paganism. The ruling
principle of her religion is terror, and her deity
is lewd and cruel. Whatever of purity the earlier
forms of paganism may have possessed, it is
evident from history that it was of brief duration.
Every form, which history has preserved, grew
rapidly and steadily worse and more corrupt,
until the entire heathen world, before the coming
of Christ, was infected with that loathsome leprosy of pollution, described with revolting vivid-
ness by St. Paul, in the beginning of his Epistle
to the Romans.

So general and decided was this proclivity
to the worship of strange gods, that, at the

time of the deluge, only one family remained
faithful to Jehovah; and this was a family which
had been favored with his special revelation.
Indeed it is evident that nothing but a revelation
from God could raise men from the degradation
of pagan idolatry, because nothing else has
ever had that effect. If man could achieve his
own freedom from this bondage, he would long
since have been free. But instead of this, the
increase of light and civilization and refinement
in the pagan world has but multiplied the objects
of his worship, added voluptuous refinements
to its ritual, and thus increased the number and
weight of his chains. In this respect there is
no difference in their moral condition, between
the barbarous Scythian and the learned Egyptian or Roman of ancient times, nor between
the ignorant African and the polished Hindu of
our own day. The only method, which has been
successfully employed to deliver man from
idolatry, is that of presenting to the eye of his
soul an object of worship perfectly holy and
pure, directly opposite, in moral character, to
the gods he had formerly adored. He could not
transfer to his deities a better character than
he himself possessed. He must forever remain
enslaved to his idols, unless a new and pure
object of worship were revealed to him, with
a display of superior power sufficient to overcome his former faith and present fears, to de-
tach his affections from grosser objects, and
to fix them upon that which alone is worthy.[6]
This is precisely what God, as stated in the Holy
Scriptures, has done. He rescued one family
from idolatry in the Old World, by the revelation
of himself to Noah; he called a distinct branch
of this family to the knowledge of himself, in
the person of Abraham and his sons; he extended

this favor to a whole nation, through the ministry of Moses; but it was through that of Jesus Christ alone that it was communicated to the whole world. In Egypt, by the destruction of all the objects of the popular worship, God taught the Israelites that he alone was the self-existent Almighty. At the Red Sea, he emphatically showed them that he was the Protector and Saviour of his people. At Sinai, he revealed himself as the righteous Governor, who required implicit obedience from men, and taught them, by the strongly-marked distinctions of the ceremonial law, that he was a holy Being, of purer eyes than to behold evil, and that could not look upon iniquity. The demerit of sin was inculcated by the solemn infliction of death upon every animal, offered as a propitiatory sacrifice. And when, by this system of instruction, he had prepared a people to receive the perfect revelation of the character of God, of the nature of his worship, and of the way of restoration to his image and favor, this also was expressly revealed by the mission of his Son.[7]

That the books of the Old Testament, as we now have them, are genuine; that they existed in the time of our Saviour, and were commonly received and referred to among the Jews, as the sacred books of their religion;[8] and that the text of the Four Evangelists has been handed down to us in the state in which it was originally written, that is, without having been materially corrupted or falsified, either by heretics or Christians; are facts which we are entitled to assume as true, until the contrary is shown.

The genuineness of these writings really admits of as little doubt, and is susceptible of as ready proof, as that of any ancient writings whatever. The rule of municipal law on this subject is familiar, and applies with equal force to all ancient writings, whether documentary or otherwise; and as it comes first in order, in the prosecution of these inquiries, it may, for the sake of mere convenience, be designated as our first rule.

Every document, apparently ancient, coming from the proper repository or custody, and bearing on its face no evident marks of forgery, the law presumes to be genuine, and devolves on the opposing party the burden of proving it to be otherwise.

An ancient document, offered in evidence in our courts, is said to come from the proper repository, when it is found in the place where, and under the care of persons with whom, such writings might naturally and reasonably be expected to be found; for it is this custody which gives authenticity to documents found within it.[9] If they come from such a place, and bear no evident marks of forgery, the law presumes that they are genuine, and they are permitted to be read in evidence, unless the opposing party is able successfully to impeach them.[10] The burden of showing them to be false and unworthy of credit, is devolved on the party who makes that objection. The presumption of law is the judgment of charity. It presumes that every man is innocent until he is proved guilty; that everything has been done fairly and legally, until it is proved to have been otherwise; and that every document, found in its proper repository, and not bearing marks of forgery, is genuine. Now this is precisely the case with the Sacred Writings. They have been used in the church from time immemorial, and thus are found in the

place where alone they ought to be looked for.
They come to us, and challenge our reception
of them as genuine writings, precisely as
Domesday Book, the Ancient Statutes of Wales,
or any other of the ancient documents which
have recently been published under the British
Record Commission, are received. They are
found in familiar use in all the churches of Chris-
tendom, as the sacred books to which all denominations of Christians refer, as the standard of
their faith. There is no pretense that they were
engraven on plates of gold and discovered in
a cave, nor that they were brought from heaven
by angels; but they are received as the plain
narratives and writings of the men whose names
they respectively bear, made public at the time
they were written; and though there are some
slight discrepancies among the copies subsequently made, there is no pretense that the originals were anywhere corrupted. If it be objected
that the originals are lost, and that copies alone
are now produced, the principles of the municipal law here also afford a satisfactory answer.
For the multiplication of copies was a public
fact, in the faithfulness of which all the Christian community had an interest; and it is a rule
of law, that,—

*In matters of public and general interest, all
persons must be presumed to be conversant,
on the principle that individuals are presumed
to be conversant with their own affairs.*

Therefore it is that, in such matters, the prevailing current of assertion is resorted to as
evidence, for it is to this that every member
of the community is supposed to be privy.[11]
The persons, moreover, who multiplied these
copies, may be regarded, in some manner, as

the agents of Christian public, for whose use
and benefit the copies were made; and on the
ground of the credit due to such agents, and
of the public nature of the facts themselves,
the copies thus made are entitled to an extraordinary degree of confidence, and, as in the case
of official registers and other public books, it
is not necessary that they should be confirmed
and sanctioned by the ordinary tests of truth.[12]
If any ancient document concerning our public
rights were lost copies which had been as universally received and acted upon as the Four Gospels have been, would have been received in
evidence in any of our courts of justice, without
the slightest hesitation. The entire text of the
Corpus Juris Civilis is received as authority in
all the courts of continental Europe, upon much
weaker evidence of its genuineness; for the integrity of the Sacred Text has been preserved
by the jealousy of opposing sects, beyond any
moral possibility of corruption; while that of
the Roman Civil Law has been preserved by
tacit consent, without the interest of any opposing school, to watch over and preserve it from
alteration.

These copies of the Holy Scriptures having
thus been in familiar use in the churches, from
the time when the text was committed to writing; having been watched with vigilance by
so many sects, opposed to each other in doctrine,
yet all appealing to these Scriptures for the correctness of their faith; and having in all ages,
down to this day, been respected as the authori-
tative source of all ecclesiastical power and
government, and submitted to, and acted under
in regard to so many claims of right, on the
one hand, and so many obligations of duty, on
the other; it is quite erroneous to suppose that

the Christian is bound to offer any further proof
of their genuineness or authenticity. It is for
the objector to show them spurious; for on him,
by the plainest rules of law, lies the burden of
proof.[13] If it were the case of a claim to a
franchise, and a copy of an ancient deed or charter were produced in support of the title, under
parallel circumstances on which to presume its
genuineness, no lawyer, it is believed, would
venture to deny either its admissibility in evidence, or the satisfactory character of the proof.
In a recent case in the House of Lords, precisely
such a document, being an old manuscript copy,
purporting to have been extracted from ancient
Journals of the House, which were lost, and to
have been made by an officer whose duty it
was to prepare lists of the Peers, was held admissible in a claim of peerage.[14]

Supposing, therefore, that it is not irrational,
nor inconsistent with sound philosophy, to believe that God has made a special and express
revelation of his character and will to man, and
that the sacred books of our religion are genuine, as we now have them; we proceed to examine and compare the testimony of Four Evangelists, as witnesses to the life and doctrines
of Jesus Christ; in order to determine the degree
of credit, to which, by the rules of evidence plied
in human tribunals, they are justly entitled. Our
attention will naturally be first directed to the
witnesses themselves, to see who and what manner of men they were; and we shall take them
in the order of their writings; stating the prominent traits only in their lives and characters,
as they are handed down to us by credible historians.

Matthew, called also Levi, was a Jew of

Galilee, but of what city is uncertain. He held the place of publican, or tax-gatherer, under the Roman government, and his office seems to have consisted in collecting the taxes within his district, as well as the duties and customs levied on goods and persons, passing in and out of his district or province, across the lake of Genesareth. While engaged in this business, at the office or usual place of collection, he was required by Jesus to follow him, as one of his disciples; a command which he immediately obeyed. Soon afterwards, he appears to have given a great entertainment to his fellow-publicans and friends, at which Jesus was present; intending probably both to celebrate his own change of profession, and to give them an opportunity to profit by the teaching of his new Master.[15] He was constituted one of the twelve apostles, and constantly attended the person of Jesus as a faithful follower, until the crucifixion; and after the ascension of his Master he preached the gospel for some time, with other apostles, in Judea, and afterwards in Ethiopia, where he died.

He is generally allowed to have written first, of all the evangelists; but whether in the Hebrew or the Greek language, or in both, the learned are not agreed, nor is it material to our purpose to inquire; the genuineness of our present Greek gospel being sustained by satisfactory evidence.[16] The precise time when he wrote is also uncertain, the several dates given to it among learned men, varying from A.D. 37 to A.D. 64. The earlier date, however, is argued with greater force, from the improbability that the Christians would be left for several years without a general and authentic history of our Saviour's ministry; from the evident allusions which it contains to a state of persecution in the church at the time it was written; from the titles of sanctity ascribed to Jerusalem, and a higher veneration testified for the temple than is found in the other and later evangelists; from the comparative gentleness with which Herod's character and conduct are dealt with, that bad prince probably being still in power; and from the frequent mention of Pilate, as still governor of Judea.[17]

That Matthew was himself a native Jew, familiar with the opinions, ceremonies, and customs of his countrymen; that he was conversant with the Sacred Writings, and habituated to their idiom; a man of plain sense, but of little learning, except what he derived from the Scriptures of the Old Testament; that he wrote seriously and from conviction, and had, on most occasions, been present, and attended closely, to the transactions which he relates, and relates, too, without any view of applause to himself; are facts which we may consider established by internal evidence, as strong as the nature of the case will admit. It is deemed equally well proved, both by internal evidence and the aid of history, that he wrote for the use of his countrymen the Jews. Every circumstance is noticed which might conciliate their belief, and every unnecessary expression is avoided which might obstruct it. They looked for the Messiah, of the lineage of David, and born in Bethlehem, in the circumstances of whose life the prophecies should find fulfillment, a matter, in their estimation, of peculiar value: and to all these this evangelist has directed their especial attention.[18]

Allusion has been already made to his employment as a collector of taxes and customs:

but the subject is too important to be passed over without further notice. The tribute imposed by the Romans upon countries conquered by their arms was enormous. In the time of Pompey, the sums annually exacted from their Asiatic provinces, of which Judea was one, amounted to about four millions and a half of sterling, or about twenty-two millions of dollars. These exactions were made in the usual forms of direct and indirect taxation; the rate of the customs on merchandise varying from an eighth to a fortieth part of the value of the commodity; and the tariff including all the principal articles of the commerce of the East, much of which, as is well known, still found its way to Italy through Palestine, as well as by the way of Damascus and of Egypt. The direct taxes consisted of a capitation-tax, and a land-tax, assessed upon a valuation or census, periodically taken under the oath of the individual, with heavy penal sanctions.[19] It is natural to suppose that these taxes were not voluntarily paid, especially since they were imposed by the conqueror upon a conquered people, and by a heathen, too, upon the people of the house of Israel. The increase of taxes has generally been found to multiply discontents, evasions and frauds on the one hand, and, on the other, to increase vigilance, suspicion, close scrutiny, and severity of exaction. The penal code, as revised by Theodosius, will give us some notion of the difficulties in the way of the revenue officers, in the earlier times of which we are speaking. These difficulties must have been increased by the fact that, at this period, a considerable portion of the commerce of that part of the world was carried on by the Greeks, whose ingenuity and want of faith were proverbial. It was to such an employment and under such circumstances, that Matthew was educated; an employment which must have made him acquainted with the Greek language, and extensively conversant with the public affairs and the men of business of his time; thus entitling him to our confidence, as an experienced and intelligent observer of events passing before him. And if the men of that day were, as in truth they appear to have been, as much disposed as those of the present time, to evade the payment of public taxes and duties, and to elude, by all possible means, the vigilance of the revenue officers, Matthew must have been familiar with a great variety of forms of fraud, imposture, cunning, and deception, and must have become habitually distrustful, scrutinizing, and cautious; and, of course, much less likely to have been deceived in regard to many of the facts in our Lord's ministry, extraordinary as they were, which fell under his observation. This circumstance shows both the sincerity and the wisdom of Jesus, in selecting him for an eye-witness of his conduct, and adds great weight to the value of the testimony of this evangelist.

Mark was the son of a pious sister of Barnabas, named Mary, who dwelt at Jerusalem, and at whose house the early Christians often assembled. His Hebrew name was John; the surname of Mark having been adopted, as is supposed, when he left Judea to preach the gospel in foreign countries; a practice not unusual among the Jews of that age, who frequently, upon such occasions, assumed a name more familiar than their own to the people whom they visited. He is supposed to have been converted to the Christian faith by the ministry of Peter. He traveled from Jerusalem to Antioch with Paul and Barnabas, and afterwards accompanied them elsewhere. When they landed at Perga in Pamphylia, he left them and returned to Jerusalem; for which reason, when he afterwards would have gone with them, Paul refused to take him. Upon this, a difference of opinion arose between the two apostles, and they separated, Barnabas taking Mark with him to Cyprus. Subsequently he accompanied Timothy to Rome, at the express desire of Paul. From this city he probably went into Asia, where he found Peter, with whom he returned to Rome, in which city he is supposed to have written and published his Gospel. Such is the outline of his history, as it is furnished by the New Testament.[20] The early historians add, that after this he went into Egypt and planted a church in Alexandria, where he died.[21]

It is agreed that Mark wrote his Gospel for the use of Gentile converts; an opinion deriving great force from the explanations introduced into it, which would have been useless to a Jew;[22] and that it was composed for those at Rome, is believed, not only from the numerous Latinisms it contains, but from the unanimous testimony of ancient writers, and from the internal evidence afforded by the Gospel itself.

Some have entertained the opinion that Mark compiled his account from that of Matthew, of which they supposed it an abridgment. But this notion has been refuted by Koppe, and others,[23] and is now generally regarded as untenable. For Mark frequently deviates from Matthew in the order of time, in his arrangement of facts; and he adds many things not related by the other evangelists; neither of which a mere epitomizer would probably have done. He also omits several things related by Matthew, and imperfectly describes others, especially the transactions of Christ with the apostles after the resurrection; giving no account whatever of his appearance in Galilee; omissions irreconcilable with any previous knowledge of the Gospel according to Matthew. To these proofs we may add, that in several places there are discrepancies between the accounts of Matthew and Mark, not, indeed, irreconcilable, but sufficient to destroy the probability that the latter copied from the former.[24] The striking coincidences between them, in style, words, and things, in other places, may be accounted for by considering that Peter, who is supposed to have dictated this Gospel to Mark, was quite as intimately acquainted as Matthew with the miracles and discourses of our Lord; which, therefore, he would naturally recite in his preaching; and that the same things might very naturally be related in the same manner, by men who sought not after excellency of speech. Peter's agency in the narrative of Mark is asserted by all ancient writers, and is confirmed by the fact, that his humility is conspicuous in every part of it, where anything is or might be related of him; his weaknesses and fall being fully exposed, while things which might redound to his honor, are either omitted or but slightly mentioned; that scarcely any transaction of Jesus is related, at which Peter was not present, and that all are related with that circumstantial minuteness which belongs to the testimony of an eye-witness.[25] We may, therefore, regard the Gospel of Mark as an original composition, written at the dictation of Peter, and consequently as another original narrative of the life, miracles, and doctrine of our Lord.

Luke, according to Eusebius, was a native of Antioch, by profession a physician, and for a considerable period a companion of the apostle Paul. From the casual notices of him in the Scriptures, and from the early Christian writers, it has been collected, that his parents were Gentiles, but that he in his youth embraced Judaism, from which he was converted to Christianity. The first mention of him is that he was with Paul at Troas;[26] whence he appears to have attended him to Jerusalem; continued with him in all his troubles in Judea; and sailed with him when he was sent a prisoner from Caesarea to Rome, where he remained with him during his two years' confinement. As none of the ancient fathers have mentioned his having suffered martyrdom, it is generally supposed that he died a natural death.

That he wrote his Gospel for the benefit of Gentile converts is affirmed by the unanimous voice of Christian antiquity; and it may also be inferred from its dedication to a Gentile. He is particularly careful to specify various circumstances conducive to the information of strangers, but not so to the Jews; he gives the lineage of Jesus upwards, after the manner of the Gentiles, instead of downwards, as Matthew had done; tracing it up to Adam, and thus showing that Jesus was the promised seed of the woman; and he marks the eras of his birth, and of the ministry of John, by the reigns of the Roman emperors. He also has introduced several things, not mentioned by the other evangelists, but highly encouraging to the Gentiles to turn to God in the hope of pardon and acceptance; of which description are the parables of the publican and pharisee, in the temple; the lost piece of silver; and the prodigal son; and the fact of Christ's visit to Zaccheus the publican, and the pardon of the penitent thief.

That Luke was a physician, appears not only from the testimony of Paul,[27] but from the internal marks in his Gospel, showing that he was both an acute observer, and had given particular and even professional attention to all our Saviour's miracles of healing. Thus, the man whom Matthew and Mark describe simply as a leper, Luke describes as *full* of leprosy;[28] he, whom they mention as having a withered hand, Luke says had his *right* hand withered;[29] and of the maid, of whom the others say that Jesus took her by the hand and she arose, he adds, that *her spirit came to her again.*[30] He alone, with professional accuracy of observation, says that *virtue went out* of Jesus, and healed the sick;[31] he alone states the fact that the sleep of the disciples in Gethsemane was *induced by extreme sorrow;* and mentions the blood-like sweat of Jesus, as occasioned by the *intensity of his agony;* and he alone relates the miraculous healing of Malchus's ear.[32] That he was also a man of a liberal education, the comparative elegance of his writings sufficiently shows.[33]

The design of Luke's Gospel was to supersede the defective and inaccurate narratives then in circulation, and to deliver to Theophilus, to whom it is addressed, a full and authentic account of the life, doctrines, miracles, death and resurrection of our Saviour. Who Theophilus was, the learned are not perfectly agreed; but the most probable opinion is that of Dr. Lardner, now generally adopted, that, as Luke wrote his Gospel in Greece, Theophilus was a man of rank in that country.[34] Either the relations subsisting between him and Luke, or the dignity and power of his rank, or both, induced the evan-

gelist, who himself also "had perfect understanding of all things from the first," to devote
the utmost care to the drawing up of a complete
and authentic narrative of these great events.
He does not affirm himself to have been an eyewitness; though his personal knowledge of some
of the transactions may well be inferred from
the "perfect understanding" which he says he
possessed. Some of the learned seem to have
drawn this inference as to them all, and to have
placed him in the class of original witnesses;
but this opinion, though maintained on strong
and plausible grounds, is not generally adopted.
If, then, he did not write from his own personal
knowledge, the question is, what is the legal
character of his testimony?

If it were "the result of inquiries, made under
competent public authority, concerning matters
in which the public are concerned," [35] it would
possess every legal attribute of an inquisition,
and, as such, would be legally admissible in
evidence, in a court of justice. To entitle such
results, however, to our full confidence, it is
not necessary that they should be obtained under
a legal commission; it is sufficient if the inquiry
is gravely undertaken and pursued, by a person
of competent intelligence, sagacity and integrity. The request of a person in authority, or
a desire to serve the public, are, to all moral
intents, as sufficient a motive as a legal commission.[36] Thus, we know that when complaint
is made to the head of a department, of official
misconduct or abuse, existing in some remote
quarter, nothing is more common than to send
some confidential person to the spot, to ascertain
the facts and report them to the department;
and this report is confidently adopted as the
basis of its discretionary action, in the correction

of that abuse, or the removal of the offender. Indeed, the result of any grave inquiry is equally certain to receive our confidence, though it may have been voluntarily undertaken, if the party making it had access to the means of complete and satisfactory information upon the subject.[37] If, therefore, Luke's Gospel were to be regarded only as the work of a contemporary historian, it would be entitled to our confidence. But it is more than this. It is the result of careful inquiry and examination, made by a person of science, intelligence and education, concerning subjects which he was perfectly competent to investigate, and as to many of which he was peculiarly skilled, they being cases of the cure of maladies; subjects, too, of which he already had the perfect knowledge of a contemporary, and perhaps an eye-witness, but beyond doubt, familiar with the parties concerned in the transactions, and belonging to the community in which the events transpired, which were in the mouths of all; and the narrative, moreover, drawn up for the especial use, and probably at the request, of a man of distinction, whom it would not be for the interest nor safety of the writer to deceive or mislead. Such a document certainly possesses all the moral attributes of an inquest of office, or of any other official investigation of facts; and as such is entitled, *in foro conscientiae*, to be adduced as original, competent and satisfactory evidence of the matters it contains.

John, the last of the evangelists, was the son of Zebedee, a fisherman of the town of Bethsaida, on the sea of Galilee. His father appears to have been a respectable man in his calling, owning his vessel and having hired servants.[38] His mother, too, was among those who followed

Jesus, and "ministered unto him;" [39] and to John himself, Jesus, when on the cross, confided the care and support of his own mother.[40] This disciple also seems to have been favorably known to the high priest, and to have influence in his family; by means of which he had the privilege of being present in his palace at the examination of his Master, and of introducing also Peter, his friend.[41] He was the youngest of the apostles; was eminently the object of the Lord's regard and confidence; was on various occasions admitted to free and intimate intercourse with him; and is described as "the disciple whom Jesus loved." [42] Hence he was present at several scenes, to which most of the others were not admitted. He alone, in company with Peter and James, was present at the resurrection of Jairus's daughter, at the transfiguration on the mount, and at the agony of our Saviour in the garden of Gethsemane.[43] He was the only apostle who followed Jesus to the cross, he was the first of them at the sepulchre, and he was present at the several appearances of our Lord after his resurrection. These circumstances, together with his intimate friendship with the mother of Jesus, especially qualify him to give a circumstantial and authentic account of the life of his Master. After the ascension of Christ, and the effusion of the Holy Spirit on the day of Pentecost, John became one of the chief apostles of the circumcision, exercising his ministry in and near Jerusalem. From ecclesiastical history we learn that, after the death of Mary the mother of Jesus, he proceeded to Asia Minor, where he founded and presided over seven churches, in as many cities, but resided chiefly at Ephesus. Thence he was banished, in Domitian's reign, to the isle of Patmos, where he wrote his Revelation. On the accession of Nerva he was freed from exile, and returned to Ephesus, where he wrote his Gospel and Epistles, and died at the age of one hundred years, about A.D. 100, in the third year of the emperor Trajan.[44]

The learned are not agreed as to the time when the Gospel of John was written; some dating it as early as the year 68, others as late as the year 98; but it is generally conceded to have been written after all the others. That it could not have been the work of some Platonic Christian of a subsequent age, as some have without evidence asserted, is manifest from references to it by some of the early fathers, and from the concurring testimony of many other writers of the ancient Christian church.[45]

That it was written either with especial reference to the Gentiles, or at a period when very many of them had become converts to Christianity, is inferred from the various explanations it contains, beyond the other Gospels, which could have been necessary only to persons unacquainted with Jewish names and customs.[46] And that it was written after all the others, and to supply their omissions, is concluded, not only from the uniform tradition and belief in the church, but from his studied omission of most of the transactions noticed by the others, and from his care to mention several incidents which they have not recorded. That their narratives were known to him, is too evident to admit of doubt; while his omission to repeat what they had already stated, or, where he does mention the same things, his relating them in a brief and cursory manner, affords incidental but strong testimony that he regarded their accounts as faithful and true.[47]

Such are the brief histories of men, whose narratives we are to examine and compare; conducting the examination and weighing the testimony by the same rules and principles which govern our tribunals of justice in similar cases. These tribunals are in such cases governed by the following fundamental rule:—

In trials of fact, by oral testimony, the proper inquiry is not whether is it possible that the testimony may be false, but whether there is sufficient probability that it is true.

It should be observed that the subject of inquiry is a matter of fact, and not of abstract mathematical truth. The latter alone is susceptible of that high degree of proof, usually termed demonstration, which excludes the possibility of error, and which therefore may reasonably be required in support of every mathematical deduction. But the proof of matters of fact rests upon moral evidence alone; by which is meant not merely that species of evidence which we do not obtain either from our own senses, from intuition, or from demonstration. In the ordinary affairs of life we do not require nor expect demonstrative evidence, because it is inconsistent with the nature of matters of fact, and to insist on its production would be unreasonable and absurd. And it makes no difference, whether the facts to be proved relate to this life or to the next, the nature of the evidence required being in both cases the same. The error of the sceptic consists in pretending or supposing that there is a difference in the nature of the things to be proved; and in demanding demonstrative evidence concerning things which are not susceptible of any other than moral evidence alone, and of which the utmost that can be said is, that there is no reasonable doubt about their truth.[48]

In proceeding to weigh the evidence of any proposition of fact, the previous question to be determined is, *when* may it be said to be proved? The answer to this question is furnished by another rule of municipal law, which may be thus stated:

A proposition of fact is proved, when its truth is established by competent and satisfactory evidence.

By competent evidence, is meant such as the nature of the thing to be proved requires; and by satisfactory evidence, is meant that amount of proof, which ordinarily satisfies an unprejudiced mind, beyond any reasonable doubt. The circumstances which will amount to this degree of proof can never be previously defined; the only legal test to which they can be subjected is, their sufficiency to satisfy the mind and conscience of a man of common prudence and discretion, and so to convince him, that he would venture to act upon the conviction in matters of the highest concern and importance to his own interest.[49] If, therefore, the subject is a problem in mathematics, its truth is to be shown by the certainty of demonstrative evidence. But if it is a question of fact in human affairs, nothing more than moral evidence can be required, for this is the best evidence which, from the nature of the case, is attainable. Now as the facts, stated in Scripture History, are not of the former kind, but are cognizable by the senses, they may be said to be proved when they are established by that kind and degree of evidence which, as we have just observed, would, in the affairs of human life, satisfy the mind and conscience of a common man. When we have this degree of evidence, it is unreasonable to require more. A juror would violate his oath, if he should refuse to acquit or condemn a person charged with an offense, where this measure of proof was adduced.

Proceeding further, to inquire whether the facts related by the Four Evangelists are proved by competent and satisfactory evidence, we are led, first, to consider on which side lies the burden of establishing the credibility of the witnesses. On this point the municipal law furnishes a rule, which is of constant application in all trials by jury, and is indeed the dictate of that charity which thinketh no evil.

In the absence of circumstances which generate suspicion, every witness is to be presumed credible, until the contrary is shown; the burden of impeaching his credibility lying on the objector.[50]

This rule serves to show the injustice with which the writers of the Gospels have ever been treated by infidels; and injustice silently acquiesced in even by Christians; in requiring the Christian affirmatively, and by positive evidence, *aliunde*, to establish the credibility of his witnesses above all others, before their testimony is entitled to be considered, and in permitting the testimony of a single profane writer, alone and uncorroborated, to outweigh that of any single Christian. This is not the course in courts of chancery, where the testimony of a single witness is never permitted to outweigh the oath even of the defendant himself, interested as he is in the cause; but, on the contrary, if the plaintiff, after having required the oath of his adversary, cannot overthrow it by something more than the oath of one witness, however credible, it must stand as evidence against him. But the Christian writer seems, by the usual course of the argument, to have been deprived of the common presumption of charity in his favor; and reversing the ordinary rule of administering justice in human tribunals, his testimony is unjustly presumed to be false, until it is proved to be true. This treatment, moreover, has been applied to them all in a body; and, without due regard to the fact, that, being independent historians, writing at different periods, they are entitled to the support of each other: they have been treated, in the argument, almost as if the New Testament were the entire production, at once, of a body of men, conspiring by a joint fabrication, to impose a false religion upon the world. It is time that this injustice should cease; that the testimony of the evangelists should be admitted to be true, until it can be disproved by those who would impugn it; that the silence of one sacred writer on any point, should no more detract from his own veracity or that of the other historians, than the like circumstance is permitted to do among profane writers; and that the Four Evangelists should be admitted in corroboration of each other, as readily as Josephus and Tacitus, or Polybius and Livy.[51]

But if the burden of establishing the credibility of the evangelists were devolved on those who affirm the truth of their narratives, it is still capable of a ready moral demonstration, when we consider the nature and character of the testimony, and the essential marks of difference between true narratives of facts and the creations of falsehoods. It is universally admitted that the credit to be given to witnesses depends chiefly on their ability to discern and comprehend what was before them, their opportunities for observation, the degree of accuracy with which they are accustomed to mark passing events, and their integrity in relating them. The rule of municipal law on this subject embraces all these particulars, and is thus stated by a legal text-writer of the highest repute.

The credit due to the testimony of witnesses depends upon, firstly, their honesty; secondly, their ability; thirdly, their number and the consistency of their testimony; fourthly, the conformity of their testimony with experience; and fifthly, the coincidence of their testimony with collateral circumstances.[52]

Let the evangelists be tried by these tests.

And *first*, as to their *honesty*. Here they are entitled to the benefit of the general course of human experience, that men ordinarily speak the truth, when they have no prevailing motive or inducement to the contrary. This presumption, to which we have before alluded, is applied in courts of justice, even to witnesses whose integrity is not wholly free from suspicion; much more is it applicable to the evangelists, whose testimony went against all their worldly interests. The great truths which the apostles declared, were that Christ had risen from the dead, and that only through repentance from sin, and faith in him, could men hope for salvation. This doctrine they asserted with one voice, everywhere, not only under the greatest discouragements, but in the face of the most appalling terrors that can be presented to the mind of man. Their master had recently perished as a malefactor, by the sentence of a public tribunal. His religion sought to overthrow the religions of the whole world. The laws of every country were against the teachings of his disciples. The interests and passions of all the rulers and great

men in the world were against them. The fashion
of the world was against them. Propagating this
new faith, even in the most inoffensive and
peaceful manner, they could expect nothing but
contempt, opposition, revilings, bitter persecutions, stripes, imprisonments, torments and
cruel deaths. Yet this faith they zealously did
propagate; and all these miseries they endured
undismayed, nay, rejoicing. As one after another
was put to a miserable death, the survivors only
prosecuted their work with increased vigor and
resolution. The annals of military warfare afford
scarcely an example of the like heroic con-
stancy, patience and unblenching courage. They
had every possible motive to review carefully
the grounds of their faith, and the evidences
of the great facts and truths which they asserted; and these motives were pressed upon their
attention with the most melancholy and terrific
frequency. It was therefore impossible that they
could have persisted in affirming the truths they
have narrated, had not Jesus actually risen from
the dead, and had they not known this fact
as certainly as they knew any other fact.[53] If
it were morally possible for them to have been
deceived in this matter, every human motive
operated to lead them to discover and avow their
error. To have persisted in so gross a falsehood,
after it was known to them, was not only to
encounter, for life, all the evils which man could
inflict, from without, but to endure also the
pangs of inward and conscious guilt; with no
hope of future peace, no testimony of a good
conscience, no expectation of honor or esteem
among men, no hope of happiness in this life,
or in the world to come.

Such conduct in the apostles would moreover
have been utterly irreconcilable with the fact,

that they possessed the ordinary constitution of our common nature. Yet their lives do show them to have been men like all others of our race; swayed by the same motives, animated by the same hopes, affected by the same joys, subdued by the same sorrows, agitated by the same fears, and subject to the same passions, temptations and infirmities, as ourselves. And their writings show them to have been men of vigorous understandings. If then their testimony was not true, there was no possible motive for this fabrication.

It would also have been irreconcilable with the fact that they were good men. But it is impossible to read their writings, and not feel that we are conversing with men eminently holy, and of tender consciences, with men acting under an abiding sense of the presence and omniscience of God, and of their accountability to him, living in his fear, and walking in his ways. Now, though, in a single instance, a good man may fall, when under strong temptations, yet he is not found persisting, for years, in deliberate falsehood, asserted with the most solemn appeals to God, without the slightest temptation or motive, and against all the opposing interests which reign in the human breast. If, on the contrary, they are supposed to have been bad men, it is incredible that such men should have chosen this form of imposture; enjoining, as it does, unfeigned repentance, the utter forsaking and abhorrence of all falsehood and of every other sin, the practice of daily self-denial, self-abasement and self-sacrifice, the crucifixion of the flesh with all its earthly appetites and desires, indifference to the honors, and hearty contempt of the vanities of the world; and inculcating perfect purity of heart and life, and intercourse of the soul with heaven. It is incredible, that bad men should invent falsehoods, to promote the religion of the God of truth. The supposition is suicidal. If they did believe in a future state of retribution, a heaven and a hell hereafter, they took the most certain course, if false witnesses, to secure the latter for their portion. And if, still being bad men, they did not believe in future punishment, how came they to invent falsehoods the direct and certain tendency of which was to destroy all their prospects of worldly honor and happiness, and to insure their misery in this life? From these absurdities there is no escape, but in the perfect conviction and admission that they were good men, testifying to that which they had carefully observed and considered, and well knew to be true.[54]

In the *second* place, as to their *ability*. The text writer before cited observes, that the ability of a witness to speak the truth, depends on the opportunities which he has had for observing the fact, the accuracy of his powers of discerning, and the faithfulness of his memory in retaining the facts, once observed and known.[55] Of the latter trait, in these witnesses, we of course know nothing; nor have we any traditionary information in regard to the accuracy of their powers of discerning. But we may well suppose that in these respects they were like the generality of their countrymen, until the contrary is shown by an objector. It is always to be presumed that men are honest, and of sound mind, and of the average and ordinary degree of intelligence. This is not the judgment of mere charity; it is also the uniform presumption of the law of the land; a presumption which is always allowed freely and fully to operate, until the fact is shown to be otherwise, by the party who denies the applicability of this presumption to the particular case in question. Whenever an objection is raised in opposition to ordinary presumptions of law, or to the ordinary experience of mankind, the burden of proof is devolved on the objector, by the common and ordinary rules of evidence, and of practice in courts. No lawyer is permitted to argue in disparagement of the intelligence or integrity of a witness, against whom the case itself afforded no particle of testimony. This is sufficient for our purpose, in regard to these witnesses. But more than this is evident, from the minuteness of their narratives, and from their history. Matthew was trained, by his calling, to habits of severe investigation and suspicious scrutiny; and Luke's profession demanded an exactness of observation equally close and searching. The other two evangelists, it has been well remarked, were as much too unlearned to forge the story of their Master's Life, as these were too learned and acute to be deceived by any imposture.

In the *third* place, as to their *number* and the *consistency* of their testimony. The character of their narratives is like that of all other true witnesses, containing, as Dr. Paley observes, substantial truth, under circumstantial variety. There is enough of discrepancy to show that there could have been no previous concert among them; and at the same time such substantial agreement as to show that they all were independent narrators of the same great transaction, as the events actually occurred. That they conspired to impose falsehood upon the world is, moreover, utterly inconsistent with the supposition that they were honest men; a fact, to the proofs of which we have already adverted. But if they were bad men, still the idea of any conspiracy among them is negatived, not only by the discrepancies alluded to, but by many other circumstances which will be mentioned hereafter; from all which, it is manifest that if they concerted a false story, they sought its accomplishment by a mode quite the opposite to that which all others are found to pursue, to attain the same end. On this point the profound remark of an eminent writer is to our purpose; that "in a number of concurrent testimonies, where there has been no previous concert, there is a probability distinct from that which may be termed the sum of the probabilities resulting from the testimonies of the witnesses; a probability which would remain, even though the witnesses were of such a character as to merit no faith at all. This probability arises from the concurrence itself. That such a concurrence should spring from chance, is as one to infinite; that is, in other words, morally impossible. If therefore concert be excluded, there remains no cause but the reality of the fact." [56]

The discrepancies between the narratives of the several evangelists, when carefully examined, will not be found sufficient to invalidate their testimony. Many seeming contradictions will prove, upon closer scrutiny, to be in substantial agreement; and it may be confidently asserted that there are none that will not yield, under fair and just criticism. If these different accounts of the same transactions were in strict verbal conformity with each other, the argument against their credibility would be much stronger. All that is asked for these witnesses is, that their testimony may be regarded as we regard the testimony of men in the ordinary affairs of life. This they are justly entitled to; and this no honorable adversary can refuse. We might, indeed, take higher ground than this, and confidently claim for them the severest scrutiny; but our present purpose is merely to try their veracity by the ordinary tests of truth, admitted in human tribunals.

If the evidence of the evangelists is to be rejected because of a few discrepancies among them, we shall be obliged to discard that of many of the contemporaneous histories on which we are accustomed to rely. Dr. Paley has noticed the contradiction between Lord Clarendon and Burnett and others in regard to Lord Strafford's execution; the former stating that he was condemned to be hanged, which was done on the same day; and the latter all relating that on a Saturday he was sentenced to the block, and was beheaded on the following Monday. Another striking instance of discrepancy has since occurred, in the narratives of the different members of the royal family of France, of their flight from Paris to Varennes, in 1792. These narratives, ten in number, and by eye-witnesses and personal actors in the transactions they relate, contradict each other, some on trivial and some on more essential points, but in every case in a wonderful and inexplicable manner.[57] Yet these contradictions do not, in the general public estimation, detract from the integrity of the narrators, nor from the credibility of their relations. In the points in which they agree, and which constitute the great body of their narratives, their testimony is of course not doubted; where they differ, we reconcile them as well as we may; and where this cannot be done at all, we follow that light which seems to us the clearest. Upon the principles of the sceptic, we should be bound utterly to disbelieve them all. On the contrary, we apply to such cases the rules which, in daily experience, our judges instruct juries to apply, in weighing and reconciling the testimony of different witnesses; and which the courts themselves observe, in comparing and reconciling different and sometimes discordant reports of the same decisions. This remark applies especially to some alleged discrepancies in the reports which the several evangelists have given of the same discourses of our Lord.[58]

In the *fourth* place, as to the *conformity of their testimony with experience.* The title of the evangelists to full credit for veracity would be readily conceded by the objector, if the facts they relate were such as ordinarily occur in human experience, and on this circumstance an argument is founded against their credibility. Miracles, say the objectors, are impossible; and therefore the evangelists were either deceivers or deceived; and in either case their narratives are unworthy of belief. Spinosa's argument against the possibility of miracles, was founded on the broad and bold assumption that all things are governed by immutable laws, or fixed modes of motion and relation, termed the laws of nature, by which God himself is of necessity bound. This erroneous assumption is the tortoise, on which stands the elephant which upholds his system of atheism. He does not inform us who made these immutable laws, nor whence they derive their binding force and irresistible operation. The argument supposes that the creator of all things first made a code of laws, and then put it out of his own power to change them. The scheme of Mr. Hume is but another form of the same error. He deduces the existence of such immutable laws from the uniform course of human experience. This, he affirms, is our only guide in reasoning concerning matters of fact; and whatever is contrary to human experience, he pronounces incredible.[59] Without stopping to examine the correctness of this doctrine, as a fundamental principle in the law of evidence, it is sufficient in this place to remark, that it contains this fallacy: it excludes all knowledge derived by inference or deduction from facts, confining us to what we derive from experience alone, and thus depriving us of any knowledge, or even rational belief, or the existence or character of God. Nay more, it goes to prove that successive generations of men can make no advancement in knowledge, but each must begin *de novo*, and be limited to the results of his own experience. But if we may infer, from what we see and know, that there is a Supreme Being, by whom this world was created, we may certainly, and with equal reason, believe him capable of works which *we* have never yet known him to perform. We may fairly conclude that the power which was originally put forth to create the world is still constantly and without ceasing exerted to sustain it; and that the experienced connection between cause and effect is but the uniform and constantly active operation of the finger of God. Whether this uniformity of operation extends to things beyond the limits of our observation, is a point we cannot certainly know. Its existence in all things that ordinarily concern us may be supposed to be ordained as conducive to our happiness; and if the belief in a revelation of peace and mercy from God is conducive to the happiness of man, it is not irrational to suppose that he would depart from his ordinary course of action, in order to give it such attestations as should tend to secure that belief. "A miracle is improbable, when we can perceive no sufficient cause, in reference to his creatures, why the Deity should not vary his modes of operation; it ceases to be so, when such cause is assigned." [60]

But the full discussion of the subject of miracles forms no part of the present design. Their credibilty has been fully established, and the objections of sceptics most satisfactorily met and overthrown, by the ablest writers of our own day, whose works are easily accessible.[61] Thus much, however, may here be remarked; that in almost every miracle related by the evangelists, the facts, separately taken, were plain, intelligible, transpiring in public, and about which no person of ordinary observation would be likely to mistake. Persons blind or crippled, who applied to Jesus for relief, were known to have been crippled or blind for many years; they came to be cured; he spake to them; they went away whole. Lazarus had been dead and buried four days; Jesus called him to come forth from the grave; he immediately came forth, and was seen alive for a long time afterwards. In every case of healing, the previous condition of the sufferer was known to all; all saw his instantaneous restoration; and all witnessed the act of Jesus in touching him, and heard his words.[62] All these, separately considered, were facts, plain and simple in their nature, easily seen and fully comprehended by persons of common capacity and observation. If they were separately testified to, by different witnesses of ordinary intelligence and integrity, in any court of justice, the jury would be bound to believe them; and a verdict, rendered contrary to the uncontradicted testimony of credible witnesses to any of these plain facts, separately taken, would be liable to be set aside, as a verdict against evidence. If one credible witness testified to the fact, that Bartimeus was blind, according to the uniform course of administering justice, this fact would be taken as satisfactorily proved. So also, if his subsequent restoration to sight were the sole fact in question, this also would be deemed established, by the like evidence. Nor would the rule of evidence be at all different, if the fact to be proved were the declaration of Jesus, immediately preceding his restoration to sight, that his faith had made him whole. In each of these cases, each isolated fact was capable of being accurately observed, and certainly known; and the evidence demands our assent, precisely as the like evidence upon any other indifferent subject. The connection of the word or the act of Jesus with the restoration of the blind, lame and dead, to sight, and health, and life, as cause and effect, is a conclusion which our reason is compelled to admit, from the uniformity of their concurrence, in such a multitude of instances, as well as from the universal conviction of all, whether friends or foes, who beheld the miracles which he wrought. Indeed, if the truth of one of the miracles is satisfactorily established, our belief cannot reasonably be withheld from them all. This is the issue proposed by Dr. Paley, in regard to the evidence of the death of Jesus upon the cross, and his subsequent resurrection, the truth of which he has established in an argument incapable of refutation.

In the *fifth* place, as to *the coincidence of their testimony with collateral and contemporaneous facts and circumstances.* After a witness is dead, and his moral character is forgotten, we can ascertain it only by a close inspection of his narrative, comparing its details with each other, and with contemporary accounts and collateral facts. This test is much more accurate than may at first be supposed. Every event which actually transpires, has its appropriate relation and place in the vast complication of circumstances, of which the affairs of men consist; it owes its origin to the events which have preceded it, is intimately connected with all others which occur at the same time and place, and often with those of remote regions, and in its turn gives birth to numberless others which succeed. In all this almost inconceivable contexture, and seeming discord, there is perfect harmony; and while the fact, which really happened, tallies exactly with every other contemporaneous incident, related to it in the remotest degree, it is not possible for the wit of man to invent a story, which, if closely compared with the actual occurrences of the same time and place, may not be shown to be false.[63] Hence it is, that a false witness will not willingly detail any circumstances, in which his testimony will be open to contradiction, nor multiply them where there is danger of his being detected by a comparison of them with other accounts, equally circumstantial. He will rather deal in general statements and broad assertions; and if he finds it necessary for his purpose to employ names and particular circumstances in his story, he will endeavor to invent such as shall be out of the reach of all opposing proof; and he will be the most forward and minute in details, where he knows that any danger of contradiction is least to be apprehended.[64] Therefore it is, that variety and minuteness of detail are usually regarded as certain tests of sincerity, if the story, in the circumstances related, is of a nature capable of easy refutation if it were false.

The difference, in the detail of circumstances, between artful or false witnesses and those who testify the truth, is worthy of especial observation. The former are often copious and even profuse in their statements, as far as these may have been previously fabricated, and in relation to the principal matter; but beyond this, all will be reserved and meagre, from the fear of detection. Every lawyer knows how lightly the evidence of a *non-mi-recordo* witness is esteemed. The testimony of false witnesses will not be uniform in its texture, but will be unequal, unnatural, and inconsistent. On the contrary, in the testimony of true witnesses there is a visible and striking naturalness of manner, and an unaffected readiness and copiousness in the detail of circumstances, as well in one part of the narrative as another, and evidently without the least regard either to the facility or difficulty of verification or detection.[65] It is easier, therefore, to make out the proof of any fact, if proof it may be called, by suborning one or more false witnesses, to testify directly to the matter in question, than to procure an equal number to testify falsely to such collateral and separate circumstances as will, without greater danger of detection, lead to the same false result. The increased number of witnesses to circumstances, and the increased number of the circumstances themselves, all tend to increase the probability of detection if the witnesses are false, because thereby the points are multiplied in which their statements may be compared with each other, as well as with the truth itself, and in the same proportion is increased the danger of variance and inconsistency.[66] Thus the force of circumstantial evidence is found to depend on the number of particulars involved in the narrative; the difficulty of fabricating them all, if false, and the great facility of detection; the nature of the circumstances to be compared, and from which the dates and other facts are to be collected; the intricacy of the comparison; the number of the intermediate steps in the process of deduction; and the circuity of the investigation. The more largely the narrative partakes of these characters, the further it will be found removed from all suspicion of contrivance or design, and the more profoundly the mind will repose on the conviction of its truth.

The narratives of the sacred writers, both Jewish and Christian, abound in examples of this kind of evidence, the value of which is hardly capable of being properly estimated. It does not, as has been already remarked, amount to mathematical demonstration; nor is this degree of proof justly demandable in any question of moral conduct. In all human transactions, the highest degree of assurance to which we can arrive, short of the evidence of our own senses, is that of probability. The most that can be asserted is, that the narrative is more likely to be true than false; and it may be in the highest degree more likely, but still be short of absolute mathematical certainty. Yet this very probability may be so great as to satisfy the mind of the most cautious, and enforce the assent of the most reluctant and unbelieving. If it is such as usually satisfies reasonable men, in matters of ordinary transaction, it is all which the greatest sceptic has a right to require; for it is by such evidence alone that our rights are determined, in the civil tribunals; and on no other evidence do they proceed, even in capital cases. Thus where a house had been feloniously broken

open with a knife, the blade of which was broken
and left in the window, and the mutilated knife
itself, the parts perfectly agreeing, was found
in the pocket of the accused, who gave no satisfactory explanation of the fact, no reasonable
doubt remained of his participation in the crime.
And where a murder had been committed by
shooting with a pistol, and the prisoner was connected with the transaction by proof that the
wadding of the pistol was part of a letter addressed to him, the remainder of which was found
upon his person, no juror's conscience could
have reproached him for assenting to the verdict
of condemnation.[67] Yet the evidence, in both
cases is but the evidence of circumstances;
amounting, it is true, to the highest degree of
probability, but yet not utterly inconsistent with
the innocence of the accused. The evidence
which we have of the great facts of the Bible
history belongs to this class, that is, it is moral
evidence; sufficient to satisfy any rational mind,
by carrying it to the highest degree of moral
certainty. If such evidence will justify the taking
away of human life or liberty, in the one case,
surely it ought to be deemed sufficient to determine our faith in the other.

All that Christianity asks of men on this subject, is, that they would be consistent with themselves; that they would treat its evidences as
they treat the evidence of other things; and that
they would try and judge its actors and witnesses, as they deal with their fellow men, when
testifying to human affairs and actions, in human tribunals. Let the witnesses be compared
with themselves, with each other, and with surrounding facts and circumstances; and let their
testimony be sifted, as if it were given in a
court of justice, on the side of the adverse party,

the witness being subjected to a rigorous cross-examination. The result, it is confidently believed, will be an undoubting conviction of their integrity, ability, and truth. In the course of such an examination, the undesigned coincidences will multiply upon us at every step in our progress; the probabilty of the veracity of the witnesses and of the reality of the occurrences which they relate will increase, until it acquires, for all practical purposes, the value and force of demonstration.

It should be remembered, that very little of the literature of their times and country has come down to us; and that the collateral sources and means of corroborating and explaining their writings are proportionally limited. The contemporary writings and works of art which have reached us, have invariably been found to confirm their accounts, to reconcile what was apparently contradictory, and supply what seemed defective or imperfect. We ought therefore to conclude, that if we had more of the same light, all other similar difficulties and imperfections would vanish. Indeed they have been gradually vanishing, and rapidly too, before the light of modern research, conducted by men of science in our own times. And it is worthy of remark, that of all the investigations and discoveries of travelers and men of letters, since the overthrow of the Roman empire, not a vestige of antiquity has been found, impeaching, in the slightest degree, the credibility of the sacred writers; but, on the contrary, every result has tended to confirm it.

The essential marks of difference between true narratives of facts and the creations of fiction, have already been adverted to. It may here be added that these attributes of truth are strikingly apparent throughout the gospel histories, and that the absence of all the others is equally remarkable. The writers allude, for example, to the existing manners and customs, and to the circumstances of the times and of their country, with the utmost minuteness of reference. And these references are never formally made, nor with preface and explanation, never multiplied and heaped on each other, nor brought together, as though introduced by design; but they are scattered broad-cast and singly over every part of the story, and so connect themselves with every incident related, as to render the detection of falsehood inevitable. This minuteness, too, is not peculiar to any one of the historians, but is common to them all. Though they wrote at different periods and without mutual concert, they all alike refer incidentally to the same state of affairs, and to the same contemporary and collateral circumstances. Their testimony, in this view, stands on the same ground with that of four witnesses, separately examined before different commissioners, upon the same interrogatories, and all adverting incidentally to the same circumstances as surrounding and accompanying the principal transaction, to which alone their attention is directed. And it is worthy of observation that these circumstances were at that time of a peculiar character. Hardly a state or kingdom in the world ever experienced so many vicissitudes in its government and political relations, as did Judea, during the period of the gospel history. It was successively under the government of Herod the Great, of Archelaus, and of a Roman magistrate; it was a kingdom, a tetrarchate, and a province; and its affairs, its laws, and the administration of justice, were all involved in the

confusion and uncertainty naturally to be expected from recent conquest. It would be difficult to select any place or period in the history
of nations, for the time and scene of a fictitious
history or an imposture, which would combine
so many difficulties for the fabricator to sur-
mount, so many contemporary writers to con-
front with him, and so many facilities for the
detection of falsehood.[68]

"Had the evangelists been false historians,"
says Dr. Chalmers, "they would not have committed themselves upon so many particulars.
They would not have furnished the vigilant in-
quirers of that period with such an effectual
instrument for bringing them into discredit with
the people; nor foolishly supplied, in every page
of their narrative, so many materials for a cross-
examination, which would infallibly have dis-
graced them. Now, we of this age can institute
the same cross-examination. We can compare
the evangelical writers with contemporary
authors, and verify a number of circumstances
in the history, and government, and peculiar
economy of the Jewish people. We therefore
have it in our power to institute a cross-
examination upon the writers of the New Testament; and the freedom and frequency of their
allusions to these circumstances supply us with
ample materials for it. The fact, that they are
borne out in their minute and incidental allusions by the testimony of other historians, gives
a strong weight of what has been called circumstantial evidence in their favor. As a specimen
of the argument, let us confine our observations
to the history of our Saviour's trial, and execution, and burial. They brought him to Pontius
Pilate. We know both from Tacitus and Josephus, that he was at that time governor of Judea.

A sentence from him was necessary before they could proceed to the execution of Jesus; and we know that the power of life and death was usually vested in the Roman governor. Our Saviour was treated with derision; and this we know to have been a customary practice at that time, previous to the execution of criminals, and during the time of it. Pilate scourged Jesus before he gave him up to be crucified. We know from ancient authors, that this was a very usual practice among Romans. The accounts of an execution generally run in this form: he was stripped, whipped, and beheaded or executed. According to the evangelists, his accusation was written on the top of the cross; and we learn from Suetonius and others, that the crime of the person to be executed was affixed to the instrument of his punishment. According to the evangelists, this accusation was written in three different languages; and we know from Josephus that it was quite common in Jerusalem to have all public advertisements written in this manner. According to the evangelists, Jesus had to bear his cross; and we know from other sources of information, that this was the constant practice of those times. According to the evangelists, the body of Jesus was given up to be buried at the request of friends. We know that, unless the criminal was infamous, this was the law or the custom with all Roman governors." [69]

There is also a striking naturalness in the characters exhibited in the sacred historians, rarely if ever found in works of fiction, and probably nowhere else to be collected in a similar manner from fragmentary and incidental allusions and expressions, in the writings of different persons. Take, for example, that of Peter, as it may be gathered from the evangelists, and it will be hardly possible to conceive that four persons, writing at different times, could have concurred in the delineation of such a character, if it were not real; a character too, we must observe, which is nowhere expressly drawn, but is shown only here and there, casually, in the subordinate parts of the main narrative. Thus disclosed, it is that of a confident, sanguine, and zealous man; sudden and impulsive, yet humble and ready to retract; honest and direct in his purposes; ardently loving his master, yet deficient in fortitude and firmness in his cause.[70] When Jesus put any question to the apostles, it was Peter who was foremost to reply,[71] and if they would inquire of Jesus, it was Peter who was readiest to speak.[72] He had the impetuous courage to cut off the ear of the High Priest's servant, who came to arrest his master; and the weakness to dissemble before the Jews, in the matter of eating with Gentile converts.[73] It was he who ran with John to the sepulchre, on the first intelligence of the resurrection of Jesus, and with characteristic zeal rushed in, while John paused without the door.[74] He had the ardor to desire and the faith to attempt to walk on the water, at the command of his Lord; but as soon as he saw the wind boisterous, he was afraid.[75] He was the first to propose the election of another apostle in the place of Judas,[76] and he it was who courageously defended them all, on the day of Pentecost, when the multitude charged them with being filled with new wine.[77] He was forward to acknowledge Jesus to be the Messiah;[78] yet having afterwards endangered his own life by wounding the servant of the High Priest, he suddenly consulted his own safety by denying the same Master, for whom, but a few hours before, he had declared himself ready to die.[79] We may safely affirm that the annals of fiction afford no example of a similar but not uncommon character, thus incidentally delineated.

There are other internal marks of truth in the narratives of the evangelists, which, however, need here be only alluded to, as they have been treated with great fullness and force by able writers, whose works are familiar to all.[80] Among these may be mentioned the nakedness of the narratives; the absence of all parade by the writers about their own integrity, of all anxiety to be believed, or to impress others with a good opinion of themselves or their cause, of all marks of wonder, or of desire to excite astonishment at the greatness of the events they record, and of all appearance of design to exalt their Master. On the contrary, there is apparently the most perfect indifference on their part, whether they are believed or not; or rather, the evident consciousness that they are recording events well known to all, in their own country and times, and undoubtedly to be believed, like any other matter of public history, by readers in all other countries and ages. It is worthy, too, of especial observation, that though the evangelists record the unparalleled sufferings and cruel death of their beloved Lord, and this too, by hands and with the consenting voices of those on whom he had conferred the greatest benefits, and their own persecutions and dangers, yet they have bestowed no epithets of harshness or even of just censure on the authors of all this wickedness, but have everywhere left the plain and unincumbered narrative to speak for itself, and the reader to pronounce his own sentence of condemnation; like true witnesses, who have nothing to gain or to lose by the event of the cause, they state the facts, and leave them to their fate. Their simplicity and artlessness, also, should not pass unnoticed, in readily stating even those things most disparaging to themselves. Their want of faith in their master, their dullness of apprehension of his teachings, their strifes for pre-eminence, their inclination to call fire from heaven upon their enemies, their desertion of their Lord in his hour of extreme peril; these and many other incidents tending directly to their own dishonor, are nevertheless set down with all the directness and sincerity of truth, as by men writing under the deepest sense of responsibility to God. Some of the more prominent instances of this class of proofs will be noticed hereafter, in their proper places, in the narratives themselves.

Lastly, the great character they have portrayed is perfect. It is the character of a sinless Being; of one supremely wise and supremely good. It exhibits no error, no sinister intention, no imprudence, no ignorance, no evil passion, no impatience; in a word, no fault; but all is perfect uprightness, innocence, wisdom, goodness and truth. The mind of man has never conceived the idea of such a character, even for his gods; nor has history or poetry shadowed it forth. The doctrines and precepts of Jesus are in strict accordance with the attributes of God, agreeably to the most exalted idea which we can form of them, either from reason or from revelation. They are strikingly adapted to the capacity of mankind, and yet are delivered with a simplicity and majesty wholly divine. He spake as never man spake. He spake with authority; yet addressed himself to the reason and the understanding of men; and he spake with wisdom, which men could neither gainsay nor resist. In his private life, he exhibits a character not merely of strict justice, but of overflowing benignity. He is temperate, without austerity; his meekness and humility are signal; his patience is invincible; truth and sincerity illustrate his whole conduct; every one of his virtues is regulated by consummate prudence; and he both wins the love of his friends, and extorts the wonder and admiration of his enemies.[81] He is represented in every variety of situation in life, from the height of worldly grandeur, amid the acclamations of an admiring multitude, to the deepest abyss of human degradation and woe, apparently deserted of God and man. Yet everywhere he is the same; displaying a character of unearthly perfection, symmetrical in all its proportions, and encircled with splendor more than human. Either the men of Galilee were men of superlative wisdom, and extensive knowledge and experience, and of deeper skill in the arts of deception, than any and all others, before or after them, or they have truly stated the astonishing things which they saw and heard.

APPENDIX B

ARTICLE

SEEKING TRUTH ON THE OTHER SIDE OF THE WALL: GREENLEAF'S EVANGELISTS MEET THE FEDERAL RULES, NATURALISM, AND JUDAS

Nancy J. Kippenhan[†]

Rules of evidence "shall be construed . . . to the end that the truth may be ascertained . . . ."[1]

"We are not afraid to follow truth wherever it may lead . . . ."[2]
~Thomas Jefferson

I. INTRODUCTION

Simon Greenleaf was one of the nineteenth century's most noted scholars in the field of evidence.[3] Although his most famous work is his *Treatise on the Law of Evidence*,[4] his most enduring and far-reaching legacy may well be his *Testimony of the Evangelists: Examined by the Rules of Evidence Administered in Courts of Justice ("Testimony")*.[5] It is as

---

[†] Assistant Professor of Law, Liberty University School of Law (B.S., M.B.A., Rensselaer Polytechnic Institute; J.D., *magna cum laude*, Widener University School of Law). I wrote this article in full recognition of the humility (some may say audacity) needed to approach Greenleaf's Testimony, and with no intent of rewriting his seminal text. My purpose is solely to introduce his acute analysis, in refreshed form, to a new generation of legal minds, "remaining always ready to give a reasoned answer to anyone who asks you to explain the hope you have in you." *1 Peter* 3:15.

1. FED. R. EVID. 102.

2. Letter from Thomas Jefferson to William Roscoe (Dec. 27, 1820), *available at* http://memory.loc.gov/ammem/collections/jefferson_papers/mtjser1.html (then follow "From May 17, 1820" to image number 419: "We are not afraid to follow truth wherever it may lead, nor to tolerate any error so long as reason is left free to combat it.").

3. Simon Greenleaf, LL.D. (1783–1853) was appointed Royall professor of law in the Law School of Harvard University from 1833 until 1846, and later succeeded Justice Joseph Story as the Dane professor of law in 1846. John Henry Wigmore, *Preface* to SIMON GREENLEAF, A TREATISE ON THE LAW OF EVIDENCE (16th ed. Little, Brown & Co. 2001) (1842).

4. GREENLEAF, *supra* note 3 (first published in 1842, dedicated by Greenleaf to the Honorable Joseph Story).

5. SIMON GREENLEAF, THE TESTIMONY OF THE EVANGELISTS: EXAMINED BY THE RULES OF EVIDENCE ADMINISTERED IN COURTS OF JUSTICE (James Cockcroft & Co. 2001) (1874) [hereinafter

significant today as it was when first published, particularly for its assertion that truth exists and can be demonstrated on both sides of the wall that has long separated the natural and the supernatural realms.

Relying on the most respected legal and theological experts of his day,[6] Greenleaf argued that the testimony of the evangelists Matthew, Mark, Luke, and John, as recorded in the four canonical gospels, would stand as credible, factual evidence in a court of law. He decried a standard of proof for religious-based sources that was higher than the standard required of evidence in secular inquiries,[7] and reminded his readers that the burden of disproving evidence lies squarely on the shoulders of the objector.[8] Greenleaf challenged his readers to approach the inquiry with "a mind free from all pride of opinion, not hostile to the truth sought for, willing to pursue the inquiry, and impartially to weigh the arguments and evidence, and to acquiesce in the judgment of right reason."[9] *Testimony* was a significant work in its time, and continues to be cited as a foundational work by those who take an evidentiary approach to Christian apologetics[10] today.[11]

TESTIMONY]. The 1874 printing contained Greenleaf's essay (pp. 1-54), accompanied by an extensive Harmony of the Gospels (pp. 55-503), where the verses of the four gospels were arranged in chronological order, providing a side-by-side comparison of the events of Jesus' life and ministry as portrayed in each gospel. The Appendix to the 1874 edition also included: Constantine Tischendorff, *The Various Versions of the Bible*; notes to each of the gospels; Simon Greenleaf, *Note on the Resurrection*; and Joseph Salvador, *The Jewish Account of the Trial of Jesus* (with an introduction by Greenleaf). The *Testimony* itself is also *available at* http://books.google.com/books?id=S3CoKC5JI3EC&printsec=frontcover&dq=testimony+of+the+evangelists&ei=BMFwSqTUCqr8ygTG4LjaDg (last visited Oct. 9, 2010).

6. In *Testimony*, Greenleaf draws from the works of many notable scholars including English lawyer and jurist Thomas Starkie (1782–1849), famous for his multi-volume *Starkie on Evidence*; Scottish mathematician and church leader Thomas Chalmers (1780–1847), who wrote *Chalmers Evidences*; and English writer and theologian Thomas Hartwell Horne (1780–1862), who filled five volumes with detailed commentary and analysis on the scriptures in his *Introduction to the Study of the Holy Scriptures*.

7. TESTIMONY, *supra* note 5, §§ 3, 27, 48.

8. *Id.* §§ 28, 33, 41.

9. *Id.* § 1.

10. "A rational defense for the existence of God . . . [using b]oth reason and scientific evidence . . . ." Louis Hoffman, *Postmodernism Dictionary*, POSTMODERNISM AND PSYCHOLOGY, http://www.postmodernpsychology.com/Postmodernism_Dictionary.html (last visited Oct. 9, 2010).

11. *See, e.g.*, PAMELA BINNINGS EWEN, FAITH ON TRIAL 52 (1999); JOSH MCDOWELL, EVIDENCE FOR CHRISTIANITY 263 (2006); LEE STROBEL, THE CASE FOR CHRIST 58 (1998).

Of course, much about the world has changed since Greenleaf penned *Testimony*. The trend toward natural philosophy, emerging from the emphasis on rational knowledge during the Enlightenment, came into sharp focus just six years after Greenleaf's death with the publication of Charles Darwin's *Origin of Species* in 1859.[12] Since then, the wall separating the natural and the supernatural has been built ever higher, foreclosing any complete definition or explanation of truth, and excluding an entire realm of potential knowledge. Generations raised and educated on a diet of naturalism now blindly accept the proposition that religious texts cannot possibly be based on fact or offer factual evidence; however, Greenleaf's *Testimony* and its progeny prove this supposition to be false, giving freedom to those who seek truth wherever it can be found.[13]

The "natural-only" approach is exemplified within naturalism's definition of science,[14] which provides "your way of knowing about the

---

12. CHARLES DARWIN, ON THE ORIGIN OF SPECIES BY MEANS OF NATURAL SELECTION, OR THE PRESERVATION OF FAVOURED RACES IN THE STRUGGLE FOR LIFE (Gryphon Editions 1987) (1859).

13. One dramatic consequence of erecting a wall between the natural and the supernatural in academia and culture is the resulting *lack* of acknowledgement of the existence of morals and sin (at least from any external source), and of sin's consequences. David Stern explains:

> We live in an age when many people do not know what sin is. Sin is violation of *Torah*, transgression of the law God gave his people in order to help them live a life which would be in their own best interests as well as holy and pleasing to God. In the so-called Age of Enlightenment, two or three centuries ago, the notion of moral relativism began to gain hold in Western societies. Under its sway people discarded the concept of sin as irrelevant. In this view there are no sins, only sickness, misfortunes, mistakes, or the outworking on one's environmental, hereditary and biological input (western terminology) or of one's fate or karma (eastern). Alternatively, sin is acknowledged to exist, but only as defined in one's culture—cultural relativism thus negates the biblical concept of sin as absolute wrong.

DAVID H. STERN, JEWISH NEW TESTAMENT COMMENTARY 17-18 (1992).

14. For example, in *Kitzmiller v. Dover Area Sch. Dist.*, 400 F. Supp. 2d 707 (M.D. Pa. 2005), the court noted that:

> [S]ince the scientific revolution of the 16th an[d] 17th centuries, science has been limited to the search for natural causes to explain natural phenomena. . . . In deliberately omitting theological or "ultimate" explanations for the existence or characteristics of the natural world, science does not consider issues of "meaning" and "purpose" in the world.

Id. at 735.

world and what ultimately exists in it."[15] Yet, evidence continues to inexorably lead the inquirer to the "primacy of facts, which is the central concern of the field of evidence. Facts are primary in any coherent study of evidence, obviously, but they are primary in an even deeper manner, for they are the foundation upon which western civilization rests."[16] *Testimony* concludes that the canonical Gospels are credible evidence, a conclusion that raises a dissonance between the demonstrable facts and an explanation that can only be found on the supernatural side of the wall.

Just as the theories of natural inquiry have changed since the initial publication of *Testimony*, so too, our knowledge about the Gospels themselves has expanded: more than 24,000 pieces of New Testament texts are now available for critical review.[17] Physical evidence consistent with the content of these documents far surpasses that of any other historical source,[18] bolstering their credibility beyond *Testimony*'s conclusions.

Since *Testimony* was first published, archeologists and historians have found evidence not only of the canonical documents themselves, but also of other ancient documents including the Dead Sea Scrolls,[19] the Nag

---

15. *Q & A on Naturalism*, CENTER FOR NATURALISM, http://www.centerfornaturalism. org/faqs.htm (last visited Oct. 9, 2010) ("Science is the basis for naturalism.").

16. Ronald J. Allen, *From the Enlightenment to Crawford to Holmes Address at the Association of American Law Schools Evidence Conference*, 39 SETON HALL L. REV. 1, 4 (2009).

17. STROBEL, *supra* note 11, at 81; *see also Preface* to IAN WILSON, JESUS: THE EVIDENCE 6-7 (1996). (This edition incorporates the "considerable number of discoveries relating to Jesus that there have been since 1984, such as the discovery of a fishing boat of his time; of the bones of the high priest Caiaphas; and of what may be the oldest known fragments of a gospel text.").

18. STROBEL, *supra* note 11, at 82 (citing F.F. BRUCE, THE BOOKS AND THE PARCHMENTS 178 (1963)) ("There is no body of ancient literature in the world which enjoys such a wealth of good textual attestation as the New Testament."); *see also* WILSON, *supra* note 17, at 23:

[W]hereas we have just a single manuscript, copied around the twelfth century, for Tacitus' history of the early Roman emperors, of canonical material alone attesting to Jesus' existence there are some 274 vellum manuscripts . . . dating from between the fourth and the eleventh centuries, and 88 papyrus fragments datable to between the second and the fourth centuries.

19. The Dead Sea Scrolls were first discovered by a Bedouin shepherd in 1947 in a cave south of Jericho. The cave contained Hebrew and Aramaic writings, along with some six hundred fragmentary inscriptions. Archeologists discovered more fragments in other caves in the region beginning in 1952. Among the numerous manuscripts and fragments were multiple sections of *Isaiah, Psalms, Jeremiah, Daniel*, and *Habakkuk*. MERRILL F. UNGER, THE DEAD SEA SCROLLS 5-7 (1957).

Hammadi tractates,[20] and more recently, tractates containing a text known as the *Gospel of Judas* ("*Judas*").[21] With each new discovery, there are many who jump to the conclusion that these new finds are reliable without any further investigation. Others use the very existence of the discovered texts as *prima facie* evidence of grand conspiracies within the early church.[22] One need look no further than the popular reaction to pop fiction such as *The Da Vinci Code*[23] or ideas from more traditional authors in "daring theories that run beyond the evidence."[24]

More than 150 years after *Testimony* was published, it is fair to ask whether Greenleaf's persuasive analytical construct would still lead today's jurists to the same conclusions. Does the testimony of the evangelists stand the test of today's evidentiary inquiry, such that it would be admitted into today's court of justice? This Article answers in the affirmative. Section II of this Article reviews Greenleaf's original analysis, updates his analytical principles to the current Federal Rules of Evidence,[25] and then applies those rules to the canonical Gospels. Section III of this Article applies the same

---

20. Bedouins discovered a cache of thirteen leather-bound volumes buried in an earthen jar near the village of Nag Hammadi in Upper Egypt in December 1945. These volumes contain fifty-two treatises that have "increased our knowledge of ancient Gnosticism immeasurably." BART D. EHRMAN, LOST CHRISTIANITIES: CHRISTIAN SCRIPTURES AND THE BATTLES OVER AUTHENTICATION 54 (2002); HERBERT KROSNEY, THE LOST GOSPEL 11 (2006).

21. *The Gospel of Judas* is one of the texts contained in a twenty-six page papyrus manuscript discovered in a cave tomb not far from the village of Qarara in Middle Egypt in the late 1970s. The Coptic document was passed on to an underground Egyptian antiquities dealer and ultimately surfaced in an antiquities market in Geneva in May 1983. KROSNEY, *supra* note 20, at 1, 9-12, 79, 106-11.

22. The term "church" in this Article is used in the context of the earliest groups of believers in Jesus. While formal orthodoxies and hierarchical organizations developed over the centuries, this Article will not focus on the issues that ultimately divided the Roman Catholic, Orthodox, Protestant, Messianic Jewish, and other denominations, but rather the gospel evidence that is foundational to them all.

23. DAN BROWN, THE DA VINCI CODE (2003). While the book's historical accuracy has been thoroughly discredited, *see, e.g.*, DARRELL L. BOCK, BREAKING THE DA VINCI CODE: ANSWERS TO THE QUESTIONS EVERYONE'S ASKING (2004); MICHAEL GREEN, THE BOOKS THE CHURCH SUPPRESSED: FICTION AND TRUTH IN THE DA VINCI CODE (2005), included in the preface is a list of items purported to be "facts," and posters for the subsequent film were subtitled with the strap line "Seek the Truth." *See, e.g.*, Tina Mrazik, *The Da Vinci Code: Seek the Truth*, ASSOCIATED CONTENT (Sept. 2, 2006), http://www.associatedcontent.com/article/56075/the_da_vinci_code_seek_the_truth.html.

24. CRAIG A. EVANS, FABRICATING JESUS: HOW MODERN SCHOLARS DISTORT THE GOSPELS 16 (2006).

25. FED. R. EVID. (2009).

critical evidentiary analysis to the non-canonical testimony of the *Gospel of Judas* to determine whether the content of that document meets the same level of credibility as the canonical Gospels. Section IV concludes with a discussion of the significance of these analyses: if the canonical Gospels are indeed credible evidence, what conclusions should be drawn from their testimony? An objective reader, coming to the question as a juror with an open mind, will find ample factual support on both sides of the wall for the truth exposited in the Gospel accounts.

II. TESTIMONY OF THE EVANGELISTS

A. Evidentiary Principles

Greenleaf's *Testimony* presents a framework with which to analyze the four canonical Gospels using the generally accepted concepts of testamentary evidence of his day. Following a line of familiar legal logic, Greenleaf first addressed the authenticity of the documents, concluding that the Gospel texts meet all of the requirements of the "ancient documents" hearsay exception.[26] Next, he established the credibility of the witnesses by examining the Gospels' authors under the same indicia of reliability used by modern courts.[27] He questioned the content and context of the testimony, evaluated the credentials and the reliability of the authors, and found them to be credible witnesses.[28] Greenleaf's final conclusion was that the four canonical Gospels would be admissible and credible in a court of law at that time.[29]

The basic evidentiary principles changed remarkably little over the subsequent century and a half. Now, as then, evidence is generally admitted for consideration unless the opposing party makes an objection, at which time the burden shifts to the opposing party to provide specific grounds for

---

26. FED. R. EVID. 803(16); TESTIMONY, *supra* note 5, § 9; *see infra* Table 1 (comparing Greenleaf's evidentiary principles to corresponding modern rules).

27. *Compare* TESTIMONY, *supra* note 5, §§ 12–25, *with* People v. Farrell, 34 P.3d 401, 406-07 (Colo. 2001) (considering factors to assess reliability of hearsay testimony). While such reliability tests do not overcome a criminal defendant's right to cross-examine witnesses against him, *Crawford v. Washington*, 541 U.S. 36 (2004), these "indicia of reliability" continue to demonstrate what it means for a witness to provide credible testimony. *See also infra* note 168, 174.

28. TESTIMONY, *supra* note 5, §§ 12-14 (analysis of Matthew as author), §§ 15–17 (Mark), §§ 18–22 (Luke), §§ 23–25 (John), §§ 29–44 (examining the credibility of the authors and the reliability of their testimony); *see also infra* Part II.B.1-2.

29. TESTIMONY, *supra* note 5, § 48.

the objection and to demonstrate that the offered evidence should not be admitted.[30] The benefit of the doubt is given to the party presenting the evidence, thus erring on the side of inclusion rather than exclusion, in order to consider the greatest amount of relevant information possible in the quest for the truth of the matter.[31] Greenleaf noted this burden on the objectors throughout *Testimony*,[32] recognizing that in the culture of that day, as today, any evidence related to a religious inquiry was "unjustly presumed to be false, until it is proved to be true,"[33] rather than accepted as true until explicitly impeached.

For Greenleaf, "[a] proposition of fact is proved, when its truth is established by competent and satisfactory evidence."[34] Such evidence is the "amount of proof, which ordinarily satisfies *an unprejudiced mind*, beyond any reasonable doubt."[35] The facts attested to in the Gospels "are cognizable by the senses, [and] may be said to be proved when they are established by that kind and degree of evidence which . . . would . . . satisfy the mind and conscience of a common man."[36] In viewing the claims of the canonical Gospels by the same standards as other evidence, Greenleaf noted:

> [T]he narrative is more likely to be true than false; and it may be in the highest degree more likely, but still be short of absolute mathematical certainty. Yet this very probability may be so great as to satisfy the mind of the most cautious, and enforce the assent of the most reluctant and unbelieving. . . . If it is such as usually satisfies reasonable men, in matters of ordinary transaction, it is all which the greatest sceptic has a right to

---

30. FED. R. EVID. 103(a)(1); TESTIMONY, *supra* note 5, §§ 8–10.

31. *See* FED. R. EVID. 401. ("'Relevant evidence' means evidence having any tendency to make the existence of any fact that is of consequence to the determination of the action more probable or less probable than it would be without the evidence."); *see also* FED. R. EVID. 402 ("All relevant evidence is admissible . . ."); FED. R. EVID. 403 (favoring admission, but excluding evidence "if its probative value is substantially outweighed by the danger of unfair prejudice"). *See* United States v. Dennis, 625 F.2d 782, 797 (8th Cir. 1980) ("In weighing the probative value of evidence against the dangers and considerations enumerated in Rule 403, the general rule is that the balance should be struck in favor of admission.").

32. *See, e.g.*, TESTIMONY, *supra* note 5, §§ 10, 28, 33.

33. *Id.* § 28.

34. *Id.* § 27.

35. *Id.* (emphasis added).

36. *Id.* (emphasis added).

require; for it is by such evidence alone that our rights are
determined, in the civil tribunals; and on no other evidence do
they proceed, even in capital cases.[37]

Speaking in the language of the time, he characterized the facts portrayed
in the canonical Gospels as moral evidence, "sufficient to satisfy any
rational mind, by carrying it to the highest degree of moral certainty."[38]
This standard remains essentially unchanged, and the Supreme Court has
cited to Greenleaf's own *Law of Evidence* in tracing the equivalence of
moral evidence, moral certainty, and reasonable doubt.[39] The Court has
noted, "We recognize that the phrase 'moral evidence' is not a mainstay of
the modern lexicon, though we do not think it means anything different
today than it did in the 19th century."[40] The Court recognized that "proof
beyond a reasonable doubt is synonymous with proof to a moral certainty,
or subjective certitude."[41] Thus, Greenleaf's standard—that the evidence
presented by the Gospel testimony rises to the same level that "will justify
the taking away of human life or liberty"[42]—remains the test of
testamentary credibility.

Greenleaf's analysis in *Testimony* was grounded in basic historical
concepts of evidentiary inquiry. As seen in the chart below, the current
federal rules are substantially identical in letter and spirit to the principles
of Greenleaf's time. Thus, when today's rules are compared with and
incorporated into Greenleaf's analysis, the conclusion must also be the
same.

---

37. *Id.* § 41.

38. *Id.*

39. *See, e.g.*, Victor v. Nebraska, 511 U.S. 1, 11-18 (1994) (citing 1 S. GREENLEAF, LAW
OF EVIDENCE 3-4 (13th ed. 1876)).

40. *Id.* at 12.

41. Stoltie v. California, 501 F. Supp. 2d 1252, 1259 (C.D. Cal. 2007) (citing Victor v.
Nebraska, 511 U.S. 1, 12 (1994)). *See generally* Steve Sheppard, *The Metamorphoses of
Reasonable Doubt: How Changes in the Burden of Proof Have Weakened the Presumption
of Innocence*, 78 NOTRE DAME L. REV. 1165 (2003); Anthony A. Morano, *A Reexamination
of the Development of the Reasonable Doubt Rule*, 55 B.U. L. REV. 507 (1975).

42. TESTIMONY, *supra* note 5, § 41.

**Table 1: Comparison of Greenleaf's Evidentiary
Principles with the Federal Rules of Evidence**

Greenleaf Rule/Principle	Modern Rule/Principle
§ 8 Every document, apparently ancient, coming from the proper repository or custody, and bearing on its face no evident marks of forgery, the law presumes to be genuine, and devolves on the opposing party the burden of proving it to be otherwise.[43]	**Rule 803. Hearsay Exceptions; Availability of Declarant Immaterial** The following are not excluded by the hearsay rule, even though the declarant is available as a witness: **(16) Statements in ancient documents** Statements in a document in existence twenty years or more the authenticity of which is established.[44] **Rule 901. Requirement of Authentication or Identification** **(a) General provision** The requirement of authentication or identification as a condition precedent to admissibility is satisfied by evidence sufficient to support a finding that the matter in question is what its proponent claims.[45] **(b) Illustrations** By way of illustration only, and not by way of limitation, the following are examples of authentication or identification conforming with the requirements of this rule: Ancient documents or data compilation. Evidence that a document or data compilation, in any form, (A) is in such condition as to create no suspicion concerning its authenticity, (B) was in a place where it, if authentic, would likely be,

---

43. *Id.* § 8.
44. FED. R. EVID. 803(16).
45. FED. R. EVID. 901(a).

	and (C) has been in existence 20 years or more at the time it is offered.[46]
§ **9** In matters of public and general interest, all persons must be presumed to be conversant, on the principle that individuals are presumed to be conversant with their own affairs.[47]	**Rule 601. General Rule of Competency** Every person is competent to be a witness except as otherwise provided by these rules.[48] **Rule 602. Lack of Personal Knowledge** A witness may not testify to a matter unless evidence is introduced sufficient to support a finding that the witness has personal knowledge of the matter. Evidence to prove personal knowledge may, but need not, consist of the witness' own testimony.[49]
§ **22** [T]he result of careful inquiry and examination, made by a person of science, intelligence and education, concerning subjects which he was perfectly competent to investigate, and as to many of which he was peculiarly skilled. . . . [50]	**Rule 702. Testimony by Experts** If scientific, technical, or other specialized knowledge will assist the trier of fact to understand the evidence or to determine a fact in issue, a witness qualified as an expert by knowledge, skill, experience, training, or education, may testify thereto in the form of an opinion or otherwise, if (1) the testimony is based upon sufficient facts or data, (2) the testimony is the product of reliable principles and methods, and (3) the witness has applied the principles and methods reliably to the facts of the case.[51]
§ **26** In trials of fact, by oral testimony, the proper inquiry is not whether it is possible that the testimony may be false, but whether there is sufficient probability that it	**No Reasonable Doubt** "Proof beyond a reasonable doubt is synonymous with proof to a moral certainty, or subjective certitude."[53]

---

46. FED. R. EVID. 901(b)(8).
47. TESTIMONY, *supra* note 5, § 9.
48. FED. R. EVID. 601.
49. FED. R. EVID. 602.
50. TESTIMONY, *supra* note 5, § 22.
51. FED. R. EVID. 702.

is true. . . . [And] that there is no reasonable doubt of their truth.[52]	"'[E]verything relating to human affairs, and depending on moral evidence, is open to some possible or imaginary doubt' – in other words, that absolute certainty is unattainable in matters relating to human affairs. Moral evidence, in this sentence, can only mean empirical evidence offered to prove such matters—the proof introduced at trial."[54]
§ 27 A proposition of fact is proved, when its truth is established by competent and satisfactory evidence.[55]	**Rule 102. Purpose and Construction** These rules shall be construed to secure fairness . . . and promotion of growth and development of the law of evidence to the end that the truth may be ascertained and proceedings justly determined.[56]
§ 28 In the absence of circumstances which generate suspicion, every witness is to be presumed credible, until the contrary is shown; the burden of impeaching his credibility lying on the objector.[57]	**Rule 601. General Rule of Competency** Every person is competent to be a witness except as otherwise provided by these rules.[58] **Rule 603. Oath or Affirmation** Before testifying, every witness shall be required to declare that the witness will testify truthfully, by oath or affirmation administered in a form calculated to awaken the witness' conscience and impress the witness' mind with the duty to do so.[59]

---

53. Stoltie v. California, 501 F. Supp. 2d 1252, 1259 (C.D. Cal. 2007).

52. TESTIMONY, *supra* note 5, § 26.

54. Victor v. Nebraska, 511 U.S. 1, 13 (1994) (quoting California jury instruction using the term "moral certainty" in its instruction regarding reasonable doubt).

55. TESTIMONY, *supra* note 5, § 27.

56. FED. R. EVID. 102.

57. TESTIMONY, *supra* note 5, § 28 (citing THOMAS STARKIE, 1 STARKIE ON EVIDENCE 514 (1842)).

58. FED. R. EVID. 601.

59. FED. R. EVID. 603.

	Rule 607. Who May Impeach The credibility of a witness may be attacked by any party, including the party calling the witness.[60]
§ 29 The credit due to the testimony of witnesses depends upon, firstly, their honesty; secondly, their ability; thirdly, their number and the consistency of their testimony; fourthly, the conformity of their testimony with experience; and fifthly, the coincidence of their testimony with collateral circumstances.[61]	**Reliability** "[W]here, when, and how the declarant made the statement, to whom the declarant made the statement, what prompted the statement, and the statement's contents all provide indicia of reliability. [Also], the nature and character of the statement, the relationship of the parties, the declarant's probable motivation for making the statement, and the circumstances surrounding the making of the statement [are] probative of the statement's trustworthiness."[62]

Table 1: Comparison of Greenleaf's Evidentiary Principles with the Federal Rules of Evidence

Moreover, Greenleaf's caution against discounting testimony due to witness bias is still sound: "If the witnesses could be supposed to have been biased, this would not destroy their testimony to matters of fact; it would only detract from the weight of their judgment in matters of opinion."[63] Thus, the evidentiary framework on which Greenleaf based his analysis of Gospel credibility remains reliable for today's jurist applying the current Federal Rules of Evidence.

---

60. FED. R. EVID. 607.

61. TESTIMONY, *supra* note 5, § 29 (citing THOMAS STARKIE, 1 STARKIE ON EVIDENCE 480, 545 (1842)).

62. People v. Farrell, 34 P.3d 401, 406 (Colo. 2001) (internal citations omitted).

63. TESTIMONY, *supra* note 5, § 30 n.1; *see, e.g.*, Saffon v. Wells Fargo & Co. Long Term Disability Plan, 522 F.3d 863 (9th Cir. 2008) ("[C]ourts are familiar with the process of weighing a conflict of interest. For example, in a bench trial the court must decide how much weight to give to a witness' testimony in the face of some evidence of bias.") (citations omitted).

B. The Testimony of the Gospels

1. Ancient Documents

An objection to these documents as hearsay evidence, and their validation under the "ancient documents" exception, remain consistent: a document more than twenty years old and whose authenticity has been established is admissible.[64] Ancient documents may be authenticated by

> [e]vidence that a document or data compilation, in any form, (A) is in such condition as to create no suspicion concerning its authenticity, (B) was in a place where it, if authentic, would likely be, and (C) has been in existence 20 years or more at the time it is offered.[65]

Few questions existed as to the authenticity of the Gospel documents in Greenleaf's time, and the archeological and historical evidence discovered since then has only reinforced the documents' authenticity.[66] While approximately 5,000 pieces of the manuscripts were available in the mid-nineteenth century, the current total is closer to 24,000.[67] Although there are no extant originals, copies date as early as 70 A.D.[68] The content of the

---

64. FED. R. EVID. 803(16).

65. FED. R. EVID. 901(8).

66. WILSON, *supra* note 17, at 16-17.

67. STROBEL, *supra* note 11, at 81.

68. *See, e.g.,* WILSON, *supra* note 17, at 21-23 (stating that manuscript fragments from the *Gospel of Matthew*, currently housed in the library at Magdalen College, Oxford, have been dated to "no later than the third quarter of the first century A.D., Pompeii and Herculaneum having been destroyed in 79 A.D. and Qumran—the site of the Dead Sea Scrolls—closed down in 70 A.D."). For copies to exist from 70 A.D., the originals would have to have been written even earlier, well within the lifetime of the eyewitnesses. If Jesus' crucifixion and resurrection date to approximately 30 A.D., then these early manuscripts came from originals written less than forty years after the events described. For perspective, the originals were written more closely in time to the events they describe than books written today about the Vietnam conflict, Martin Luther King, Jr., or landing a man on the moon. John's Gospel, generally dated near the end of the first century, is likewise analogous to Steven Spielberg's Shoah project, founded in 1994 to record the eyewitness testimonies of those who survived the Nazi Holocaust of the 1930s and '40s. *See* SURVIVORS OF THE SHOAH VISUAL HISTORY FOUNDATION, http://college.usc.edu/vhi/aboutus/ (last visited Oct. 30, 2010). Richard Bauckham also compares the vivid events of the Holocaust to the equally vivid events of Jesus' ministry, death, and resurrection. RICHARD BAUCKHAM, JESUS AND THE EYEWITNESSES 493-505 (2006).

copies across the centuries is identical in all but the smallest details, leaving the fundamental testimony of the individual authors unchanged.[69]

Such consistency throughout the archeological record adds support to the acceptance of this testimony through the ancient documents exception. The basic premise behind the exception is that, unless there is reason to suspect forgery or tampering, the contents of a document of sufficient age are most likely to be the original contents and, therefore, trustworthy.[70] Greenleaf relied on this premise, maintaining that

> the text of the Four Evangelists has been handed down to us in the state in which it was originally written, that is, without having been materially corrupted or falsified, either by heretics or Christians; are facts which we are entitled to assume as true, until the contrary is shown.[71]

The canonical Gospels have been accepted as genuine narratives of the life of Jesus since they were written in the first century, and were found in the marketplace of that day, where they would have been expected to be found. As Greenleaf noted:

> There is no pretense that they were engraven on plates of gold and discovered in a cave,[72] nor that they were brought from

---

69. *See* STROBEL, *supra* note 11, at 75-76 (quoting Strobel's interview with Bruce M. Metzger, Ph.D.):

[W]hat the New Testament has in its favor, especially when compared with other ancient writings, is the unprecedented multiplicity of copies that have survived. . . .

. . . .

[T]he more often you have copies that agree with each other, especially if they emerge from different geographical areas, the more you can cross-check them to figure out what the original document was like. . . .

. . . .

. . . We have copies commencing within a couple of generations from the writings of the originals, whereas in the case of other ancient texts, maybe five, eight, or ten centuries elapsed between the original and the earliest surviving copy.

70. *See* Threadgill v. Armstrong World Indus., 928 F.2d 1366, 1375-76 (3d Cir. 1991) (noting that the only questions for the trial judge are: (1) Were the documents in question what they purported to be? and (2) Do they purport to have been in existence twenty years or more?).

71. TESTIMONY, *supra* note 5, § 8.

72. There is a certain amount of irony in Greenleaf's comments here. Fragments of canonical Gospel manuscripts are often found in excavations of living areas of the relevant time period, where they would have been read and relied on in everyday life and study;

heaven by angels; but they are received as the plain narratives
and writings of the men whose names they respectively bear,
made public at the time they were written; and though there are
some slight discrepancies among the copies subsequently made,
there is no pretense that the originals were anywhere corrupted.[73]

Thus, no genuine concern exists regarding the authenticity of the texts.

2. The Witnesses

If the documents themselves are authentic, what can be said of the
credibility of their authors, the witnesses to the events as portrayed in those
documents? As with Greenleaf, "[o]ur attention will naturally be first
directed to the witnesses themselves, to see who and what manner of men
they were . . . ."[74] The Federal Rules of Evidence presume that any person
is competent to be a witness,[75] but also require evidence "sufficient to
support a finding that the witness has personal knowledge of the matter."[76]
The credibility of a witness may be challenged as to his character for
truthfulness,[77] but "[e]vidence of the beliefs or opinions of a witness on
matters of religion is not admissible for the purpose of showing that by
reason of their nature the witness' credibility is impaired or enhanced."[78]
The most accepted understanding of the authors has not changed since
Greenleaf's analysis:

[T]he uniform testimony of the early church was that Matthew,
also known as Levi, the tax collector and one of the twelve
disciples, was the author of the first gospel in the New
Testament; that John Mark, a companion of Peter, was the author
of the gospel we call Mark; and that Luke, known as Paul's

---

however, documents that were generally not viewed as authentic by early believers (e.g.,
Gnostic texts such as those found at Nag Hammadi and the *Gospel of Judas*) have more
often been found in caves.

73. TESTIMONY, *supra* note 5, § 9.

74. *Id.* § 11.

75. FED. R. EVID. 601.

76. FED. R. EVID. 602.

77. FED. R. EVID. 608(a).

78. FED. R. EVID. 610. In the discussion in Section III, *infra*, for example, the credibility
of the author of *Judas* should not be questioned simply because he was Gnostic. The content
and truth of his writings can, however, be examined and challenged on their veracity.

"beloved physician," wrote both the gospel of Luke and the Acts of the Apostles.[79]

The first three Gospels have generally been dated to the middle of the first century, possibly as early as the late 30s,[80] with John's writings ascribed to his time in exile at the end of that century.[81] All were written by men who were alive at the time of the events they recorded, in close physical and geographical proximity to the people, places, and events they describe, and "within living memory of the events they recount."[82] Two of the authors—Matthew and John—were *talmidim*[83] of Jesus, personally

---

79. STROBEL, *supra* note 11, at 26-27 (quoting an interview with Craig L. Blomberg, Ph.D.). This understanding mirrors that of the early church:

> Matthew published his own Gospel among the Hebrews in their own tongue, when Peter and Paul were preaching the Gospel in Rome and founding the church there. After their departure, Mark, the disciple and interpreter of Peter, himself handed down to us in writing the substance of Peter's preaching. Luke, the follower of Paul, set down in a book the Gospel preached by his teacher. Then John, the disciple of the Lord, who also leaned on his breast, himself produced his Gospel while he was living at Ephesus in Asia.

Id. at 29 (citing IRENAEUS, ADVERSUS HAERESES 3.3.4).

80. TESTIMONY, *supra* note 5, § 12. *See generally supra* note 68 (discussion of dates of Gospel texts). Corroboration for mid-century originals is provided by Luke's *Book of Acts*, which was written after his Gospel and devoted primarily to the careers of Peter and Paul, and to the growth of the early church. While *Acts* includes a number of historical dates, e.g., the succession of Porcius Festus as procurator of Judea c. 59 A.D. while Paul was a prisoner in Caesarea, there is no mention of the deaths of Paul or Peter (mid-60s A.D.), or the death of James (c. 62 A.D.). The Jewish War with the Romans that began in 66 A.D., and the fall of Jerusalem in 70 A.D., are also absent. These events would have been central to the book's key persons and geography, making them integral to its theme, and their absence argues for an earlier date for the original Gospel testimonies, before the mid-60s. *See also* KEITH F. NICKLE, THE SYNOPTIC GOSPELS 85, 129, 159 (2001). Moreover, *Acts* ends abruptly; it does not say what happened to Paul. Blomberg suggests this is likely because Paul had not yet been executed. So, *Acts* "cannot be dated any later than A.D. 62." *Luke* came before *Acts*, and *Mark* likely came before *Luke*, perhaps the late 50s or 60 at the latest. STROBEL, *supra* note 11, at 42 (citing Strobel's interview with Craig L. Blomberg, Ph.D.); *see also* Luke's preface to *Acts*, citing his Gospel: "In the first book, I wrote about everything Yeshua set out to do and teach." *Acts* 1:1.

81. F.F. BRUCE, JESUS & CHRISTIAN ORIGINS OUTSIDE THE NEW TESTAMENT 16 (1974) (dating John's Gospel between 90 and 100 A.D.); CRAIG L. BLOMBERG, THE HISTORICAL RELIABILITY OF JOHN'S GOSPEL: ISSUES AND COMMENTARY 41-42 (2002) (noting a consensus among scholars dating c. 95 A.D.).

82. BAUCKHAM, *supra* note 68, at 7.

83. *Talmidim* (Hebrew; singular: *talmid*) were a rabbi's disciples or students whose desire was not only to know what their teacher knew, but to also become like him. RAY VANDER LAAN, ECHOES OF HIS PRESENCE 50 (1998); *see also* STERN, *supra* note 13, at 23:

present for what they recount.[84] Mark is generally accepted to have been a recording secretary of another of Jesus' disciples, Peter.[85] And Luke, while not one of the original twelve disciples, was a first-generation author who spent significant time with the first-century witnesses and teachers. The precise details and the historical accounts, both in Luke's Gospel and in his *Book of Acts*, are sufficient to demonstrate his personal knowledge, as well as to corroborate, and be corroborated by, other sources. "In the absence of circumstances which generate suspicion, every witness is to be presumed credible, until the contrary is shown; the burden of impeaching his credibility lying on the objector."[86]

As one of the first disciples called by Jesus, Matthew was an eyewitness to Jesus' life and ministries.[87] As a Jew, Matthew was "familiar with the opinions, ceremonies, and customs of his countrymen . . . conversant with the Sacred Writings, and habituated to their idiom . . . ."[88] His gospel was written for a Jewish audience, and reflects the scripture and idiom of his people. But Matthew was also a tax collector,[89] considered beneath contempt in that time. David Stern explains that "Jews who undertook to collect taxes for the Roman rulers were the most despised people in the Jewish community. Not only were they serving the oppressors, but they found it easy to abuse the system so as to line their own pockets by exploiting their fellow Jews."[90] Perhaps more important to an analysis of Matthew's credibility, his position would have made Matthew a skeptic, "familiar with a great variety of the forms of fraud, imposture, cunning, and deception, and [he] must have become habitually distrustful, scrutinizing, and cautious . . . ,"[91] certainly not the type of man who would blindly

---

The English word "disciple" fails to convey the richness of the relationship between a rabbi and his *talmidim* in the first century . . . [*Talmidim*] wholeheartedly gave themselves over to their teachers (though not in a mindless way, as happens today in some cults). The essence of the relationship was one of trust in every area of living, and its goal was to make the *talmid* like his rabbi in knowledge, wisdom and ethical behavior.

84. BAUCKHAM, *supra* note 68, at 417-18.

85. *Id.* at 235.

86. TESTIMONY, *supra* note 5, § 28 (citing STARKIE, *supra* note 57, at 16, 480, 521).

87. *See generally id.* §§ 12-15.

88. *Id.* § 13.

89. *Matthew* 9:9 (DAVID H. STERN, COMPLETE JEWISH BIBLE: AN ENGLISH VERSION OF THE *TANAKH* (OLD TESTAMENT) AND *B'RIT HADASHAH* (NEW TESTAMENT) 1223-62 (1998)) [hereinafter Complete Jewish Bible].

90. STERN, *supra* note 13, at 30; *see also* TESTIMONY, *supra* note 5, § 8.

91. TESTIMONY, *supra* note 5, § 14.

follow any of the numerous prophets or zealots who promised political freedom.

Instead, Matthew's testimony is that of a humble man, with no bragging or boasting of his own position, but rather telling the story of a man whom Matthew fully believed fulfilled the role of the promised messiah. Matthew's text traces Jesus' lineage from Abraham to David, from David to the Babylonian Exile, from the exile to "the Messiah."[92] In a few short verses, Matthew summarizes two thousand years of Jewish history and promise, placing Jesus in the context of the meta-narrative of God's covenant with his people; nowhere is the progression from promise to fulfillment more succinctly displayed than here.[93]

By comparison, Mark's text, generally considered "an original composition, written at the dictation of Peter,"[94] was written primarily for a Gentile audience. Mark transcribed Peter's oral teaching,[95] and "puts readers into direct touch with Peter's oral teaching. By doing more than translate, Mark puts readers in touch with a primary source, Peter's eyewitness testimony."[96] Peter is most prevalent in Mark's Gospel,[97] most notable in the beginning and ending of the text, "form[ing] an *inclusio* around the whole story, suggesting that Peter is the witness whose testimony includes the whole. This is striking confirmation . . . that Peter was the source of the Gospel traditions in Mark's Gospel."[98] As Peter's

---

92. *Matthew* 1:1-17; *cf.* Smith's description of the universality of Matthew's genealogy (and, by implication, of the offering of salvation through Jesus):

[I]n Jesus' early roots are not only such notable righteous men as Abraham and David, but also several who stand out in history as being particularly unrighteous, including wicked King Manasseh. Not only are there Jews, . . . but also Gentiles, including a Canaanite and a Moabite, whose respective countrymen have been notorious enemies of God's people.

F. LAGARD SMITH, THE DAILY BIBLE 1353 (1996). The list also included women, two of whom (Tamar and Rahab), "are known best for sins which they had committed." *Id.*

93. Matthew's incorporation of Jewish texts is most readily apparent in a format that highlights these passages within the text of the Gospel. *See, e.g.*, Complete Jewish Bible 1223-62. *See also id.* at xliii-xlvii (list of *Tanakh* prophesies fulfilled by Jesus); *id.* at 1610-15 (index of *Tanakh* passages cited in the New Testament); STERN, *supra* note 13, at 79-80 (prophesies of how the Messiah will die and where these prophecies were fulfilled by Jesus); STERN, *supra* note 13, at 81-82 (discussion of God's covenants).

94. TESTIMONY, *supra* note 5, §§ 15–17.

95. BAUCKHAM, *supra* note 68, at 221.

96. *Id.* at 208-10.

97. *Id.* at 125-27, 148-49 tbl. 11 (noting persons named in Mark's Gospel).

98. *Id.* at 125.

transcriptionist, Mark includes testimony from a number of events where Peter was present with James and John, but not with the other disciples.[99] As in Matthew's text, Mark's testimony provides a human portrayal of the disciples, including his source, Peter, not as

> an aged apostle reminiscing expansively in autobiographical mode, but an apostle fulfilling his commission to preach the Gospel and to teach believers, relating the traditions he has been recounting throughout his life as an apostle in the forms in which he had cast the memories of the Twelve and himself for ease of teaching and communication.[100]

Mark's text provides a glimpse into "a story of personal transformation through failure, self-recognition and restoration (the latter something to which Mark's narrative points, without recounting it), a dramatic example of the encounter with the meaning of the cross . . . ."[101] Thus, by recording Peter as the source and using him as the most demonstrative character, Mark's Gospel is an eyewitness recollection of Jesus. "Though acknowledging Jesus as Son of God, Mark is quite candid about [Jesus'] human nature. The moods and emotions he ascribed to Jesus are richer and more varied than in any of the other canonical Gospels. Jesus becomes angry, tires, hungers, groans, pities, and wonders."[102] Mark's Gospel relates —as only eyewitness testimony could—the humanity of Jesus as experienced by one of his closest companions.

Such personal testimony from the original witnesses was extremely important to those in the early church, including Papias,[103] who wrote from Hierapolis that he preferred speaking with the apostles, "for I did not imagine that things out of books would help me as much as the utterances of a living and abiding voice."[104] Based on his discussions with the eyewitnesses, Papias determined that Mark had

---

99. *See, e.g., Mark* 5:22-37 (raising Jairus's daughter); *Mark* 9:2 (Jesus' transfiguration); *Mark* 14 (in Gethsemane before Jesus' arrest).

100. BAUCKHAM, *supra* note 68, at 172.

101. *Id.* at 179-80.

102. NICKLE, *supra* note 80, at 69 (citing *Mark* 1:41; 3:5; 4:13; 5:30, 32; 6:6, 34; 7:17; 8:2, 12, 33; 10:14, 21; 11:12; 14:33; 15:34, 37).

103. BAUCKHAM, *supra* note 68, at 208-10.

104. NICKLE, *supra* note 80, at 188. "Papias wrote this in the preface to a lost five-volume collection of Jesus sayings. Eusebius quoted from the preface in his History of the Church from Christ to Constantine 3:39:2-3, p. 150." *Id.* at 208 n.21.

> reproduced in his Gospel exactly what he heard Peter say. . . .
> Mark intended to do no more than write down what Peter said just
> as he recalled it. This emphasis coheres much more naturally with
> calling Mark Peter's "translator" than with conceding Mark
> freedom to interpret what Peter said.[105]

Further, Papias found that "Mark 'made no mistake' and did not include 'any false statement.' And Papias said Matthew had preserved the teachings of Jesus as well."[106] Thus, both Mark and Matthew, writing with different styles to serve the needs of different audiences, testify to the same events as portrayed in their respective Gospels.

Likewise, John wrote for a still-young Gentile church, but one that was already familiar with the testimonies of Matthew, Mark, and Luke, as well as the letters of Paul.[107] John's reader is presumed to have previous knowledge of the material in the Synoptic[108] Gospels.[109] Thus, his testimony does not dwell on details already provided by others, but his "relating [the other Gospels] in a brief and cursory manner, affords incidental but strong testimony that he regarded their accounts as faithful and true."[110]

John was the self-described disciple Jesus "particularly loved"[111] and was "present at several scenes, to which most of the others were not admitted."[112] John, his brother James, and Peter were present at the

---

105. BAUCKHAM, *supra* note 68, at 205.

106. STROBEL, *supra* note 11, at 28 (citing interview with Craig L. Blomberg, Ph.D.).

107. TESTIMONY, *supra* note 5, § 25:

> That it was written either with especial reference to the Gentiles, or at a period
> when very many of them had become converts to Christianity, is inferred from
> the various explanations it contains, beyond the other Gospels, which could
> have been necessary only to persons unacquainted with Jewish names and
> customs.

108. The first three Gospels in canon order (Matthew, Mark, Luke) are often referred to as "synoptic," reflecting that the similarities among the three allow them to be "'viewed together' (that is what 'synoptic' means) in a comparative way." NICKLE, *supra* note 80, at 42-43.

109. For example, when John describes the raising of Lazarus from the dead (*John* 11), the apostle begins by refreshing the reader's recollection that this is Bethany, where Jesus and the disciples stayed after the triumphal entry into Jerusalem (*Mark* 11:11-12), and where Mary and Martha lived (*Luke* 10:38-42), and that Mary was the same woman who washed Jesus' feet with her hair (*Luke* 7:38). STERN, *supra* note 13, at 189.

110. TESTIMONY, *supra* note 5, § 23, 25.

111. *E.g.*, *John* 13:23, 21:20 (Complete Jewish Bible).

112. TESTIMONY, *supra* note 5, § 23.

resurrection of Jairus' daughter,[113] at the transfiguration on the mount,[114] and with Jesus in the garden of Gethsemane.[115] John and Peter followed Jesus to the palace of the high priest after Jesus was arrested.[116] John was the only disciple expressly reported to be with Jesus at the cross,[117] and he was the first disciple at the empty tomb.[118] John was also present on the occasions when Jesus appeared after Jesus' resurrection.[119]

John's testimony was written at the end of the first century as one of the last eyewitness accounts.[120] Papias attributed much of his understanding to his discussions with "the Elder," which referred to John.[121] While John's work often complements the Synoptic Gospels, and in some cases adds details,[122] John chose "the incidents he reports to suit his purpose."[123] While "there are also many other things Jesus did,"[124] John "recognize[d] the value of brevity (compare *Ecclesiastes* 12:12)."[125]

John provides a particularly personal and loving perspective of the life and work of Jesus.[126] Exclusively in John's testimony, we hear Jesus' final exhortation to his *talmidim* before his arrest and crucifixion, and just before

---

113. *Mark* 5:37 (Jesus took only Peter, James, and John to Jairus' home).

114. *Matthew* 17:1; *Mark* 9:2; *Luke* 9:28.

115. *See Matthew* 26:36-37; *Mark* 14:32-33; *Luke* 22:39; *John* 18:1.

116. *John* 18:15.

117. *John* 19:25-27:

> Near the cross of Jesus stood his mother, his mother's sister, Mary Magdalene. When Jesus saw his mother there, and the disciple whom he loved standing nearby, he said to his mother, "Dear woman, here is your son," and to the disciple, "Here is your mother." From that time on, this disciple took her into his home.

118. *John* 20:2-10.

119. *John* 20:21-21:25; *see also Matthew* 28:16-20; *Mark* 16:14-20; *Luke* 24:13-49.

120. TESTIMONY, *supra* note 5, § 24.

121. BAUCKHAM, *supra* note 68, at 202-04; *see also II John* 1:1, *III John* 1:1 (beginning with "From: The Elder").

122. STERN, *supra* note 13, at 206 (indentifying "one of the men" (*Matthew* 26:51) with Jesus when he was arrested as Peter; the "servant of the [high priest]" (*Mark* 14:47) was named Malchus; Jesus' comment to Peter regarding the cup he is about to drink corresponds to the prayers in Gethsemane (*Luke* 22:42)).

123. *Id.* at 213.

124. *John* 21:25.

125. STERN, *supra* note 13, at 213.

126. TESTIMONY, *supra* note 5, § 23.

taking the short walk[127] across the Kidron Valley to Gethsemane.[128] Jesus knows what is about to happen to him. John's testimony conveys urgency as Jesus reminds his friends that Jesus alone is the vine, that they must stay united with him to produce fruit, and that they must love one another—just as he has loved them.[129] Looking back from the end of the century, John relates Jesus' foreshadowing of the persecution to come: "No one has greater love than a person who lays down his life for his friends."[130] And the reassurance: "You are my friends, if you do what I command you. . . . I have called you friends, because everything I have heard from my Father I have made known to you."[131] Yet again: "This is what I command you: keep loving each other!"[132] These inclusions, in particular, embody the witness of John, the disciple Jesus loved, "testifying about these things and who has recorded them."[133]

The final gospel witness testimony comes from Luke, the author of both the third Synoptic Gospel and the *Book of Acts*.[134] Known as a physician[135] and a traveling companion of Paul,[136] Luke provides not only a particularized account of the life of Jesus, but also a detailed history of the early church.[137] Luke was the objective observer.[138] His testimonies were

---

127. Approximately a half-mile. STERN, *supra* note 13, at 217 (noting that the distance from the Old City to the Mount of Olives falls within the rabbinic rules for walking on Shabbat).

128. *John* 18.

129. *John* 15:1-11.

130. *John* 15:13.

131. *John* 15:14-15. Jesus as loving friend "is not the common image of Christianity. God forgive us, we have smothered the risen Christ in denominationalism, ecclesiasticism, respectability, moralism, and goodness knows what else. But that is the heart of authentic Christianity." MICHAEL GREEN, THE DAY DEATH DIED 79 (1982).

132. *John* 15:17.

133. *John* 21:24.

134. *See generally* TESTIMONY, *supra* note 5, §§ 18–22; STERN, *supra* note 13, at 215.

135. *Colossians* 4:14 (referring to "our dear friend, Luke, the doctor"); *cf.* NICKLE, *supra* note 80, at 142 ("Scholars often have claimed that the large amount of technical medical vocabulary in *Luke-Acts* strongly supports the thesis that the author was a physician. . . . [This] only establishes that he was well educated, not that he was, necessarily, a doctor.").

136. TESTIMONY, *supra* note 5, § 18; *see, e.g., Acts* 20-28; *Philemon* 24.

137. BAUCKHAM, *supra* note 68, at 115. *See generally Acts*.

138. TESTIMONY, *supra* note 5, § 20.

written for a Gentile audience, [139] and although his writing style was Greek, Luke may have been Jewish. [140]

The preface to Luke's Gospel explains his purpose in providing further testimony: "Luke knew of other accounts already written, but, much as he admired them and had learned from them, he considered them to be inadequate for the needs of his own community." [141] While Luke was a schooled man and a skilled writer, the "details of the preface . . . belong to no Greek literary tradition as such but are idiosyncrasies reflecting Christian or biblical modes of speech." [142] Writing to Theophilos, Luke explains:

> [M]any people have undertaken to draw up accounts based on what was handed down to us by *those who from the start were eyewitnesses* and proclaimers of the message. Therefore, Your Excellency, since *I have carefully investigated all these things from the beginning*, it seemed good to me that I too should write you an accurate and ordered narrative, so that you might know how well-founded are the things about which you have been taught. [143]

In the same manner, Luke prefaces *Acts*, again to Theophilos: "In the first book, I wrote about everything Yeshua set out to do and teach, until the day when, after giving instructions through the [Holy Spirit] to the emissaries whom he had chosen, he was taken up into heaven." [144] *Acts* forms the sequel to Luke's Gospel testimony; "they are two parts of a single

---

139. *Id.* § 19. For example, Luke's genealogy of Jesus is traced upward in the Gentile style. *Compare Luke* 3:23-38 *with Matthew* 1:1-17. Luke uses the progression of Roman officials to provide contemporary corroboration for his events. Also, Luke dedicates both of his texts to "Theophilos," generally considered to have been an upper-class Greek. STERN, *supra* note 13, at 103. "Alternatively, since the name means "lover of God," Luke may be writing to a generic and typical disciple." STERN, *supra* note 13, at 103.

140. *E.g.*, *Acts* 27:9 (recording the time of Paul's final journey to Rome as occurring "past the Fast," i.e., after Yom Kippur. STERN, *supra* note 13, at 320. This dating "lends strength to the contention that Luke himself was Jewish or a proselyte to Judaism; he would otherwise be unlikely to measure time for his Gentile reader (1:1-4) by the Jewish calendar." *Id.*).

141. NICKLE, *supra* note 80, at 146.

142. LOVEDAY ALEXANDER, THE PREFACE TO LUKE'S GOSPEL: LITERARY CONVENTION AND SOCIAL CONTEXT IN LUKE 1.1-4 AND ACTS 1.1 103 (Margaret E. Thrall ed., 1993).

143. *Luke* 1:1-4 (Complete Jewish Bible) (emphasis added).

144. *Acts* 1:1-2 (Complete Jewish Bible).

literary work. Luke composed them as a unity, intending that they be read together. The prefaces to the two volumes make this plain."[145]

In *Acts*, Luke was often a participant in the events he describes, whereas his Gospel testimony is based on the accounts handed down by eyewitnesses after Luke personally gathered and investigated them. What legal significance does Luke's writing have in this current inquiry? Greenleaf, among others,[146] placed Luke in the role of an "expert witness" who used his finely tuned powers of observation as a physician to describe in his Gospel the life of Jesus, as well as in his *Acts of the Apostles* the life of the early church, in which he was an active participant. His testimony "is the result of careful inquiry and examination, made by a person of science, intelligence and education, concerning subjects which he was perfectly competent to investigate, and as to many of which he was peculiarly skilled . . . ."[147] In examining the style and content of Luke's work, Loveday Alexander makes similar observations, noting that "[L]uke fits specifically into the practice of the later scientific writers . . . . [h]is language is simple and modest, and there are no excessive claims."[148] Comparing his work to other historians and writers of the same time period, "Luke's preface is significantly closer to those of the scientific writers—especially to those of

---

145. NICKLE, *supra* note 80, at 136; *see also* SAMUEL BYRSKOG, STORY AS HISTORY – HISTORY AS STORY: THE GOSPEL TRADITION IN THE CONTEXT OF ANCIENT ORAL HISTORY 228-29 (2000) (comparing Luke's two volumes with a similar arrangement and similar prefaces in Josephus' two-volume work *Contra Apionem*).

146. TESTIMONY, *supra* note 5, § 22; *see also* BAUCKHAM, *supra* note 68, at 117 ("[T]he form and rhetoric of Luke's preface much more closely resemble those of prefaces to technical or professional treatises (for example, handbooks on medicine, mathematics, engineering, or rhetorical theory) than those of prefaces to historical works.").

147. TESTIMONY, *supra* note 5, § 22 (stating the standard for expert testimony at that time). The current federal rule is comparable:

> If scientific, technical, or other specialized knowledge will assist the trier of fact to understand the evidence or to determine a fact in issue, a witness qualified as an expert by knowledge, skill, experience, training, or education, may testify thereto in the form of an opinion or otherwise, if (1) the testimony is based upon sufficient facts or data, (2) the testimony is the product of reliable principles and methods, and (3) the witness has applied the principles and methods reliably to the facts of the case.

FED. R. EVID. 702; *see, e.g.*, United States v. Members of the Estate of Boothby, 16 F.3d 19, 22-23 (1st Cir. 1994) (noting that even though the witness was not a nautical architect, she was sufficiently familiar with both the regulations and the vessel at issue to qualify as an expert).

148. ALEXANDER, *supra* note 142, at 147 (observing that Luke's introduction parallels "the prefaces of Hero of Alexandria, which date from around A.D. 70—which is, of course, well within the range of dates probable for Luke's literary activity").

his contemporary Hero of Alexandria—than to any other group, and his links with the scientific tradition go deeper than the mere adoption of a conventional form of words."[149]

Moreover, Luke's Gospel and *Acts* both demonstrate the type of close scrutiny and attention to detail to be expected from a man trained in a scientific discipline. It is counter-intuitive to believe that Luke would have spent his life in defense of an endeavor for which he did not find substantial evidence. Both books are integrated not only into the historical and scientific facts of the day, but also into the meta-narrative of the fulfillment of God's promises to humankind:

> It is possible to know the data of history—people, places, dates, events—and still be ignorant of, or even hostile to, God's design of redemption. But secular history provides the context into which God inserts God's saving presence. In that context the divine plan for salvation unfolds. . . . [Luke] wanted to integrate the story of Jesus' life and the history of the church into a comprehensive understanding of God's redemptive history unfolding in secular history.[150]

This integration, coupled with the collaborative support of secular history, adds to the credibility of the writers and their testimony.

3. Content and Context

Understanding and evaluating any of the gospels "requires us to think both in terms of the historical setting of Jesus and the historical setting of the [human] authors."[151] The veracity of the Gospel writers is further buttressed by the corroboration evidenced among their reports, and by the comparison of those reports to known historical facts and circumstances.[152] Greenleaf noted, "[a]fter a witness is dead, and his moral character is forgotten, we can ascertain it only by a close inspection of his narrative, comparing its details with each other, and with contemporary accounts and

---

149. *Id.* at 202; *see also id.* at 148-64 (examining similar authors of the time: "This combination of secular Greek preface-convention [leading into] biblical narrative immediately calls to mind the literature of hellinistic Judaism, where we find a comparable mixture: biblical narrative or discourse is embellished with stylistic features reminiscent of Greek literature.").

150. NICKLE, *supra* note 80, at 153.

151. GORDON D. FEE & DOUGLAS STUART, HOW TO READ THE BIBLE FOR ALL ITS WORTH 130 (3d ed. 2003).

152. *See generally* TESTIMONY, *supra* note 5, §§ 29–47 (referring to ability of witnesses, corroboration, discrepancies, naturalness of writing, and consistent treatment of evidence).

collateral facts."[153] Even the minor discrepancies among the testimonies provide additional credibility to the individual witness of each author.[154] If, as might be suggested by challengers, the four were merely copied one from the other, or from a common source document, or written in concert, the details would likely be more identical.[155] While the Gospels, especially considered in parallel, show overwhelming similarities and agreements, they also show the minor deviations that would be expected from multiple eyewitness accounts. The 1847 edition containing *Testimony* also included extensive tables showing how and where the events of the respective testimonies were reported in the other texts, and providing a framework to view the overwhelming similarities among them.[156]

The credibility of the testimonies can be assessed by examining the breadth, the harmony, and the antiquity of the four Gospels, both among themselves and in comparison to what is considered credible from other secular sources.[157] Secular historians of the day often wrote from a greater distance in time than did the Gospel witnesses. "Tacitus . . . wrote some eighty years after most of the events he described, yet his accuracy is rated very highly."[158] Suetonius wrote 100 years after the events he described, and the Jewish book of Maccabees, written seventy years after the exploits of the freedom fighters, is considered "a most reliable document."[159] In recognizing how the accounts complement and corroborate each other, particularly in comparison to secular historical sources, Greenleaf asserted that "the Four Evangelists should be admitted in corroboration of each other, as readily as Josephus and Tacitus, or Polybius and Livy . . . ."[160]

---

153. TESTIMONY, *supra* note 5, § 39.

154. *Id.* § 34.

155. *Id.*

156. TESTIMONY, *supra* note 5, tbl. at ix ("Contents and Synopsis of the Harmony"). The similarities are particularly notable in a printing of the Gospels where the content of the four is integrated into one. *See* SMITH, *supra* note 92, at 1350-51 (integrating the four sets of "recorded events as nearly as possible in their proper chronological sequence . . . [provides] . . . a new sense of context and an added appreciation of the significance of each separate event within that context."); BAUCKHAM, *supra* note 68, at 285-86 ("We may reasonably suppose that the extent of variation we can observe in the extant records (the canonical Gospels along with the early extracanonical material) is the same—no greater or less—as the extent to which the traditions varied in oral performance.").

157. GREEN, *supra* note 131, at 35-36.

158. *Id.* at 36.

159. *Id.*

160. TESTIMONY, *supra* note 5, § 28; *see also* BAUCKHAM, *supra* note 68, at 8-10 ("The ancient historians—such as Thucydides, Polybius, Josephus, and Tacitus—were convinced

Challenges to the content of the gospel testimony often come from those who question the purported miracles, generally from those relying on their own limited human experience or natural observation.[161] Greenleaf addresses such arguments, particularly those of Spinoza and Hume, which are echoed by today's naturalists.[162] Moreover, Greenleaf notes that "[i]n almost every miracle related by the evangelists, the facts, separately taken, were plain, intelligible, transpiring in public, and about which no person of ordinary observation would be likely to mistake."[163] But because the wall between the natural and the secular remains in place, Greenleaf's admonitions for objective consideration are as necessary and as applicable today as they were then:

> If [the miraculous events] were separately testified to, by different witnesses of ordinary intelligence and integrity, in any court of justice, the jury would be bound to believe them; and a verdict, rendered contrary to the uncontradicted testimony of credible witnesses to any one of these plain facts, separately taken, would be liable to be set aside, as a verdict against evidence.[164]

Here, the corroborated—and unrefuted—experience of the Gospel writers and, indeed, thousands of other eyewitnesses reported to have been present, would be credible under any legal analysis. "In each of these cases, each isolated fact was capable of being accurately observed, and certainly known; and the evidence demands our assent, precisely as the like evidence upon any other indifferent subject."[165] After nearly two thousand years, the testimony of the Gospel writers has not been effectively challenged. Greenleaf concluded that "[e]ither the men of Galilee were men of superlative wisdom, and extensive knowledge and experience, and of deeper skill in the arts of deception, than any and all others, before or after them, or they have truly stated the astonishing things which they saw and heard."[166]

---

that true history could be written only while events were still within living memory . . . the historian had also to rely on eyewitnesses whose living voices he could hear and whom he could question himself . . . .").

161. TESTIMONY, *supra* note 5, § 38.

162. *Id.* § 37 n.1 (citing Lord Brougham's two-point refutation of Hume's argument).

163. *Id.* § 38.

164. *Id.*

165. *Id.*

166. *Id.* § 48.

Greenleaf's tests of the credibility of the authors' statements include those that would still be recognized in any court of law: "The credit due to the testimony of witnesses depends upon, firstly, their honesty; secondly, their ability; thirdly, their number and the consistency of their testimony; fourthly, the conformity of their testimony with experience; and fifthly, the coincidence of their testimony with collateral circumstances."[167] For today's courts to determine whether a statement "bears the particularized guarantees of trustworthiness necessary to justify its admission, [the courts] examine the totality of the circumstances surrounding the making of the statement . . . . [and] should predicate [the] reliability determination on an examination of the circumstances surrounding the making of the statement."[168] Greenleaf's tests and modern courts' methods of assessing reliability are wholly compatible.

The testimony of the witnesses in their Gospels reflects their own experience and observations, whether the eyewitness testimony of Matthew, Peter (through Mark), and John, or the expert investigations of Luke. Psychological studies have identified a number of factors that contribute to the quality and reliability of recollective memory, including, whether the account involves a unique or unusual event, a salient or consequential event, an event in which a person in emotionally involved, or vivid imagery.[169] Similarly, courts use well-established factors every day to determine the reliability of testimony:

> [W]here, when, and how the declarant made the statement, to whom the declarant made the statement, what prompted the statement, and the statement's contents all provide indicia of reliability. [In addition], the nature and character of the statement, the relationship of the parties, the declarant's probable motivation for making the statement, and the circumstances

---

167. *Id.* § 29.

168. People v. Farrell, 34 P.3d 401, 406 (Colo. 2001) (citations omitted); *see also* Washington v. Crawford, No. 25307-1-II, 2001 Wash. App. LEXIS 1723 (Wash. Ct. App. July 30, 2001), *rev'd*, 541 U.S. 36 (2004). While the holdings of *Farrell* and *Crawford* vis-à-vis testimonial statements made without benefit of cross-examination were challenged by *Crawford v. Washington*, 541 U.S. 36 (2004), the lower courts' discussions of the reliability of witness testimony reflects an established understanding of what makes such testimony reliable. "There are countless factors bearing on whether a statement is reliable; the nine-factor balancing test applied by the Court of Appeals below is representative." *Crawford*, 541 U.S. at 63.

169. BAUCKHAM, *supra* note 68, at 330-35; *see also id.* at 493-505 (comparing Gospel testimony to Holocaust testimony as credible reporting of exceptional events).

surrounding the making of the statement [are] probative of the statement's trustworthiness.[170]

In sum, the "ability of a witness to speak the truth, depends on the opportunities which he has had for observing the fact, the accuracy of his powers of discerning, and the faithfulness of his memory in retaining the facts, once observed and known."[171]

In similar fashion, the Supreme Court has relied on a nine-part analysis for reliability that "examines factors that show particularized guaranties of the statement's trustworthiness,"[172] essentially the same as those relied on by Greenleaf:[173]

> [W]hether the declarant had an apparent motive to lie . . . whether the declarant's general character suggests trustworthiness . . . whether more than one person heard the statement . . . whether the declarant made the statement spontaneously . . . whether the timing of the statements and the relationship between the declarant and the witness suggests trustworthiness . . . whether [the] statement contained express assertions of past fact . . . whether cross-examination could help to show the declarant's lack of knowledge . . . [whether] the event was remote . . . [and] whether the circumstances surrounding the statement suggest that the declarant misrepresented the defendant's involvement.[174]

By nineteenth century standards and those of the current Federal Rules of Evidence, the writers provide credible testimony. Greenleaf proposes that the inquirer

> [l]et the witnesses be compared with themselves, with each other, and with surrounding facts and circumstances; and let their testimony be sifted, as if it were given in a court of justice, on the side of the adverse party, the witness being subjected to a

---

170. *Farrell*, 34 P.3d at 406 (internal citations omitted).

171. TESTIMONY, *supra* note 5, § 33 (citing STARKIE, *supra* note 57, at 483, 548).

172. *Crawford*, 541 U.S. at 63 (2004) (discussing tests for reliability in, *inter alia*, *Crawford*, 2001 Wash. App. LEXIS 1723 at *12 (citations omitted)).

173. TESTIMONY, *supra* note 5, § 47.

174. *Crawford*, 2001 Wash. App. LEXIS 1723 at *13-16. *See generally supra* note 168. The credibility and reliability of the Gospel testimony are supported by traditional tests of reliability. Moreover, their content has withstood nearly two millennia of cross-examination by historic, archaeological, and cultural opponents. *See generally* STROBEL, *supra* note 11.

> rigorous cross-examination. The result, it is confidently believed,
> will be an undoubting conviction of their integrity, ability, and
> truth.[175]

Testimony conducted a thorough and complete examination of the four Gospels using Greenleaf's factors. The standards remain unchanged; the conclusion must also remain unchanged. Greenleaf noted in particular that in these "true witnesses there is a visible and striking naturalness of manner."[176] In comparing the testimony among the four, along with external corroborating historical data, he concluded that the accounts provide "substantial truth, under circumstantial variety,"[177] with "no possible motive for [] fabrication."[178]

Most important, in "all the investigations and discoveries of travelers and men of letters, since the overthrow of the Roman empire, not a vestige of antiquity has been found, impeaching, in the slightest degree, the credibility of the sacred writers; but, on the contrary, every result has tended to confirm it."[179] This remains as true today as it was when Greenleaf first penned his *Testimony*. "[T]he longer people explore this, the more details get confirmed. Within the last hundred years archaeology has repeatedly unearthed discoveries that have confirmed specific references in the gospels."[180]

Moreover, external corroboration from historical documents and archeological evidence supports the fundamental credibility of the witnesses. The writings of historians, such as Josephus,

> bear[] witness to Jesus's date, to his being the brother of James
> the Just, to his reputation as a miracle-worker, to his crucifixion
> under Pilate as a consequence of charges brought against him by
> the Jewish rulers, to his claim to be the Messiah, and to his being
> the founder of the "tribe of Christians."[181]

Works by the second generation of church authors attest to their investigation of the original sources. Papias in particular noted:

---

175. TESTIMONY, *supra* note 5, § 42.

176. *Id.* § 40.

177. *Id.* § 34.

178. *Id.* § 31.

179. *Id.* § 43.

180. STROBEL, *supra* note 11, at 64-65 (citing an interview with Craig L. Blomberg, Ph.D.).

181. F.F. BRUCE, JESUS & CHRISTIAN ORIGINS OUTSIDE THE NEW TESTAMENT 40-41 (1974).

And if by chance anyone who had been in attendance on the elders should come my way, I inquired about the words of the elders—[that is,] what [according to the elders] Andrew or Peter said (*eipen*), or Philip, or Thomas or James, or John or Matthew or any other of the Lord's disciples, and whatever Aristion and the elder John, the Lord's disciples, were saying (*legousin*).[182]

The credibility and corroboration have also survived the intervening century and a half of "classical form criticism's confidence in its ability to reconstruct the oral prehistory of the texts in detail."[183] Today's scholars are returning to the "study of cultural context—a type of investigation that was foreign to classical form criticism."[184] Historical events (for example the persecutions under Caligula in 39-41 A.D. and the Jewish War in 66-74 A.D.) add context to the Gospels and corroborate the details of their testimony.[185] Moreover, such events add factual, secular evidence that should be readily acceptable on both sides of the natural/supernatural wall, and certainly evidence that further verifies the credibility of the Gospel testimony in any legal inquiry.

Greenleaf's analytical framework and the rules of evidence both then and now support the credibility of the witness provided by the canonical Gospels. How, then, does the *Gospel of Judas* compare to the *Gospels of Matthew, Mark, Luke,* and *John*? If the four have been established as credible, is *Judas* unreliable simply based on its facial inconsistencies with the others? The following section again uses Greenleaf's analytic construct, this time to examine *Judas* and judge its credibility.

III. THE GOSPEL OF JUDAS

"Over the years the sands of Egypt have surrendered countless treasures and archaeological wonders, and now they have yielded another spectacular find: the Gospel of Judas . . ."[186]

---

182. BAUCKHAM, *supra* note 68, at 293-94 (citing EUSEBIUS, HIST. ECCL. 3.39.3-4); *see supra* notes 103-06, 121 and accompanying text (noting Papias' discussion of *Mark*).

183. GERD THEISSEN, THE GOSPELS IN CONTEXT: SOCIAL AND POLITICAL HISTORY IN THE SYNOPTIC TRADITION 2 (Linda M. Maloney trans., 1991).

184. *Id.*; *see also* BAUCKHAM, *supra* note 68, at 246-49; NICKLE, *supra* note 80, at 18-21.

185. THEISSEN, *supra* note 183, at 258-81; *see also* STERN, *supra* note 13, at 305 (citing Josephus *Antiquities of the Jews* in corroboration/explanation of arrival of "the Egyptian" cited in *Acts* 21:38).

186. THE GOSPEL OF JUDAS 7 (Rodolphe Kasser, Marvin Meyer & Gregor Wurst eds., 2006).

A. The Document

In the spring of 2006, the National Geographic Society released an English translation of a papyrus manuscript known as the *Gospel of Judas*.[187] The release of the translation of this third-century tractate was staged with a very twenty-first century marketing campaign, the type that seems to accompany the frequent pre-Easter "astonishing" finds that challenge traditional Christian doctrine.[188] *Judas* is a Gnostic[189] text, most

---

187. *See, e.g.*, Andrew Cockburn, *The Judas Gospel*, NAT'L GEOGRAPHIC (May 2006),http://ngm.nationalgeographic.com/2006/05/judas-gospel/cockburn-text. *See also* Laurie Goodstein, *Document is Genuine, but is its Story True?*, N.Y. TIMES (Apr. 7, 2006), http://www.nytimes.com/2006/04/07/us/07gospel.html. Photographs of the tractate, the Coptic transcription, and National Geographic's English translations are available online at http://www.nationalgeographic.com/lostgospel/document.html (last visited Nov. 1, 2010).

188. Easter, 2010, occasioned another such revelation. *See The Real Face of Jesus?*, HISTORY.COM, http://www.history.com/shows/the-real-face-of-jesus/articles/about-the-real-face-of-jesus (last visited Nov. 1, 2010). In 2002, the *cause célèbre* was the discovery of the purported burial box of Jesus' brother James. *See, e.g.*, Hillary Mayell, *Burial Box May Be That of Jesus's Brother, Expert Says*, NAT'L GEOGRAPHIC NEWS (Oct. 21, 2002), http://news.nationalgeographic.com/news/2002/10/1021_021021_christianrelicbox.html. National Geographic announced the find in October of 2002, followed by a flurry of media discussion about the box just in time for Easter 2003. *See, e.g.*, Roger Highfield & Jonathan Petre, *Burial box "held the bones of Jesus's brother"*, THE TELEGRAPH (Apr. 18, 2003), http://www.telegraph.co.uk/news/worldnews/northamerica/canada/1427854/Burial-box-held-the-bones-of-Jesuss-brother.html; Ben Witherington III & Hershel Shanks, *In the Name of the Brother*, USA WEEKEND, Apr. 11-13, 2003, at 8-9. Experts declared the artifact a "fake" later that year. Hillary Mayell, *"Jesus Box" Is a Fake, Israeli Experts Rule*, NAT'L GEOGRAPHIC NEWS (June 18, 2003), http://news.nationalgeographic.com/news/2003/06/0618_030618_jesusbox.html. Sensationalism also shows itself in the editing of such materials. In the preface to the second edition of his book *Jesus: The Evidence*, Ian Wilson noted:

> When the first edition of this book was written back in 1984, it was as an accompaniment to London Weekend Television's subsequently notorious three-part television series of the same name. In the course of my working together with the series' makers it became apparent that they had some quite difference ideas from my own regarding what constituted a properly objective approach to the historical Jesus.

WILSON, *supra* note 17.

189. *Gnostic/Gnosticism*: from the Greek *gnosis* (meaning "knowledge"). The terms refer not to the pursuit of general knowledge but to a variety of religious movements directed toward personal salvation through attainment of knowledge of alleged ancient mysteries (usually pertaining to self-knowledge or awareness). As such, Gnosticism represents a variety of religious movements, many of which borrowed ideas from multiple sources and closely resembled aspects of ancient mystery religions, Zoroastrianism, Platonism, and Stoicism.

THE POPULAR ENCYCLOPEDIA OF APOLOGETICS 234 (Ed Hindson & Ergun Caner eds., 2008).

likely written in the early- to mid-second century.[190] Its tone and content are similar to other Gnostic documents, several copies of which were found in 1945 near Nag Hammadi, Egypt.[191] When author Dan Brown spun his *Da Vinci Code* tale, he relied on a number of the Nag Hammadi texts, treating them as of equal (or greater) credibility than canonical sources, without any analytical examination or confirmation to justify such recognition.[192]

Although copies of these documents have been found only relatively recently, the contents were well known at the time of their writing, and throughout the centuries since. Greenleaf himself references the apocryphal *Gospel of the Infancy*.[193] Early church scholars distinguished these Gnostic documents from the eyewitness accounts of the gospels that were ultimately accepted as canon.[194] By the time *Judas* was written, nearly a century after the eyewitness accounts, "most experts agree, a 'Gospel' said more about the group that produced it than about the facts of Jesus' life and death or even the understandings of his earliest followers."[195] Herbert Krosney

---

190. APRIL D. DeCONICK, THE THIRTEENTH APOSTLE: WHAT THE GOSPEL OF JUDAS REALLY SAYS 4 (2007); *see also* KASSER ET AL., *supra* note 186, at 11; JAMES M. ROBINSON, THE SECRETS OF JUDAS 78 (2006). The *Gospel of Judas* was likely written around 150 A.D., as were several other Gnostic writings including the *Apocalypse of Adam*, and *Hypostasis of the Archons*. In contrast, Paul's epistles were written between 49 and 62 A.D., *Matthew*, *Mark*, *Luke* and *Acts* were written between 60 and 90 A.D., and the *Gospel of John* is estimated to have been written between 90 and 100 A.D. *See, e.g.*, APRIL D. DeCONICK, THE THIRTEENTH APOSTLE xiv-xv (comparatively dating "Early Christian History" with "New Testament and Sethian Gnostic Texts"); *see also* WILSON, *supra* note 17, tbl. at 17; *see generally supra* notes 68, 80 discussing the dates of the Gospels.

191. *See, e.g.*, THE NAG HAMMADI LIBRARY, http://www.nag-hammadi.com/ (last visited Aug 14, 2010).

192. BROWN, *supra* note 23, at 266 (citing, e.g., the *Gospel of Philip*).

193. TESTIMONY, *supra* note 5, § 9. *See generally* EHRMAN, *supra* note 20, at 146-62 (discussing various texts referred to generally as "infancy gospels"). Similar texts include the *Gospel of Truth*, a Gnostic text that "does not relate stories about the life, death, and resurrection of Jesus. Instead, it celebrates the 'good news' of the salvation that Jesus has brought by revealing the knowledge that can lead to deliverance from this material world." *Id.* at 83.

194. These early church writers have been referred to as "heresiologists" or "heresy hunters," and included Irenaeus, Tertullian, and Hippolytus of Rome. EHRMAN, *supra* note 20, at 54; *see also* HINDSON ET AL., *supra* note 189, at 233. Prior to the Nag Hammadi discoveries, "[c]hurch fathers such as Justin Martyr (d. 165), Irenaeus (d. c. 225), Clement of Alexandria (d. c. 215)[,] Tertullian (d. c. 225), Hippolytus (d. c. 236), Origen (d. c. 254), and Epiphanius (d. 403) provide the most important non-Gnostic references to Gnostic leaders and beliefs.".

195. David Van Biema, *A Kiss for Judas*, TIME (Feb. 19, 2006), http://www.time.com/time/magazine/article/0,9171,1161238,00.html.

detailed the trail of *Codex Tchacos*, the tractate that contained the *Gospel of Judas*, along with three other documents.[196] He describes the atmosphere that likely surrounded the creation of this particular document:

> Within this context of turbulence—between 330 and 380—the final framework of the Christian canon crystallized. It represented a significant step toward a defined single body of holy literature that was recognized by all Christians. Athanasius played the critical role in achieving this unified vision. In his thirty-ninth festal letter, written in 367, he basically defined what was acceptable and what was not. He gave his stamp of approval to the New Testament, *as it was already generally formulated.*
>
> In his letter, which was read throughout Egypt in Christian churches, Athanasius delineated the canon: These are the four Gospels, according to Matthew, Mark, Luke, and John. . . ."[197]

While *The Da Vinci Code* and its adherents portray the final canonization as yet another grand conspiracy,[198] Athanasius' letter merely provided recognition of what the church body at large already knew: the four Gospels chosen for the final canon contained the proven testimony of eyewitnesses, which is far preferable to alternative, speculative, and unsubstantiated texts proposed by other groups, including the Gnostic sects in Egypt.[199]

The National Geographic translation[200] portrays Judas Iscariot not as the evil, greedy "betrayer" of Jesus, or the pariah depicted in the canonical

---

196. KROSNEY, *supra* note 20.

197. *Id.* at 200 (emphasis added); *see also* STROBEL, *supra* note 11, at 90 (citing an interview with Bruce M. Metzger, Ph.D.):

[T]he canon was not the result of a series of contests involving church politics. The canon is rather the separation that came about because of the intuitive insight of Christian believers. They could hear the voice of the Good Shepherd in the gospel of John; they could hear it only in a muffled and distorted way in the Gospel of Thomas, mixed in with a lot of other things.

198. *See, e.g.*, BROWN, *supra* note 23, at 250-51 (portraying selection of canon as political ploy by the Emperor Constantine).

199. See Lee Strobel's discussion with Bruce Metzger regarding the formation of the canon. STROBEL, *supra* note 11, at 86, 90.

200. Since the initial release of *Judas*, National Geographic has also released photographs and texts of the tractates and their transcriptions. A debate has arisen among Coptic scholars as to the accuracy of those portions of the translation that show Judas in a favorable light. For purposes of the analysis in this article, the exact translation is not critical, as the evidentiary analysis focuses on the author's credibility. If the author is not credible, the text becomes inconsequential in pursuit of the truth. *See* DECONICK, *supra* note

Gospels, but rather as a close and trusted confidant of Jesus who was the only one of the twelve disciples to truly understand what Jesus' death would accomplish.[201] But this concept of Judas as a necessary player in the crucifixion story is hardly new, nor does it challenge traditional Christian orthodoxy.[202]

The remainder of *Judas*, however, depicts an understanding of creation, the universe, and the relationship to a single deity not generally accepted by the world's Abrahamic religions. Rather than the monotheism evidenced in Judaism and Christianity,[203] the Gnostics believed that the creator of the human universe was just one of many divine beings, working in one of many realms.[204] These beliefs bear striking resemblance to the heavenly realms of the Platonic construct.[205] Indeed, there is a discernable progression from the Platonic realms to the Gnostic knowledge-based ideology, to the Enlightenment's challenge to "dare to know" with the "freedom to use one's own intelligence,"[206] all presupposing that one's own

---

190; *see also* April D. DeConick, *Gospel Truth*, N.Y. TIMES (Dec. 1, 2007), *available at* http://www.nytimes.com/2007/12/01/opinion/01deconink.html; Marvin Meyer, *On the Waterfront with Judas*, NAT'L GEOGRAPHIC, http://press.nationalgeographic.com/pressroom/index.jsp?pageID=pressReleases_detail&siteID=1&cid=1196942552919 (last visited Nov. 1, 2010); M. J. Jacobsen, *Statement from National Geographic in Response to April DeConic's New York Times Op-Ed "Gospel Truth,"* NAT'L GEOGRAPHIC (Dec. 1, 2007), http://press.nationalgeographic.com/pressroom/index.jsp?pageID=pressReleases_detail&siteID=1&cid=1196944434958.

201. KASSER ET AL., *supra* note 186. An annotated translation appears at pages 17-45 and the remainder of the volume includes essays discussing the tractate, the translation, and the significance of the find. Photographs of the tractate, along with the Coptic transcription and National Geographic's English translations, are also available online at http://www.nationalgeographic.com/lostgospel/document.html (last visited Nov. 1, 2010).

202. *See Matthew* 26:14, 24-25 (Judas identified as the betrayer of Jesus); *see also Acts* 1:16-20 (Judas' betrayal fulfilled Jewish prophecy).

203. These Gnostic sects and writings pre-date by five centuries the rise of another monotheistic religion, Islam, which was founded in the early- to mid-600s. HINDSON ET AL., *supra* note 189, at 278-79.

204. DECONICK, *supra* note 190, at 25, 32-33.

205. *Id.* at 27.

206. Allen, *supra* note 16, at 6. Kant's theme is best captured in his opening paragraph: Enlightenment is man's emergence from self-imposed immaturity for which he himself was responsible. Immaturity and dependence are the inability to use one's own intellect without the direction of another. One is responsible for this immaturity and dependence, if its cause is not a lack of intelligence, but a lack of determination and courage to think without the direction of another. *Sapere aude! Dare to know!* is therefore the slogan of the Enlightenment.

intelligence will not lead to a monotheistic God. Today's naturalists are quick to accept at face value documents that purport to challenge traditional sacred orthodoxy, even though such documents provide far less natural proof for their suppositions than the eyewitness testimony of the Gospels. Heavenly realms are certainly more speculative and conjectural—and the rest of the documents thus more suspect and less credible—than the eyewitness experiences of thousands of first-century Judeans as related in the canonical Gospels.

B. *Evidentiary Analysis*

1. *Judas* is Also an Ancient Document

Like the canonical Gospels, there is little doubt that the papyrus on which the copy of *Gospel of Judas* was written is authentic, dating to between A.D. 220 and 340.[207] The papyrus and the leather binding have been dated using radiocarbon dating,[208] and similar scientific analysis revealed the ink to be consistent with inks of that time period, possibly an "iron-gall ink that included a small amount of carbon black (soot). If so, it could be a previously unknown 'missing link' between the ancient world's carbon-based inks and the iron-gall alternatives that became popular in medieval times."[209] The National Geographic team also examined the document for handwriting, text, and context, and determined that a "modern forger would not be able to duplicate such a document."[210]

The tractate's physical authenticity is also supported in part by historical references. The content of a "Judas Gospel" was addressed by Irenaeus in his *Refutation of All Heresies*, written in Lyon, France in or about A.D. 180.[211] Irenaeus credited the work to a Cainite Gnostic sect:

Id. (quoting Immanuel Kant, *An Answer to the Question: What is Enlightenment?* (1784), *reprinted in* KANT: POLITICAL WRITINGS 54 (H.S. Reiss ed., H.B. Nisbet trans., 2nd ed. 1991)). *See also* DECONICK, *supra* note 190, at 25-28.

207. *See generally Authentication*, NAT'L GEOGRAPHIC, http://www.nationalgeographic.com/lostgospel/authentication.html (last visited Nov. 1, 2010).

208. *Radiocarbon Dating*, NAT'L GEOGRAPHIC, http://www.nationalgeographic.com/lostgospel/auth_dating.html (last visited Nov. 1, 2010).

209. *Ink Analysis*, NAT'L GEOGRAPHIC, http://www.nationalgeographic.com/lostgospel/auth_ink.html (last visited Nov. 1, 2010).

210. *Paleography*, NAT'L GEOGRAPHIC, http://www.nationalgeographic.com/lostgospel/auth_paleo.html (last visited Nov. 1, 2010). *See also Contextual Evidence*, NAT'L GEOGRAPHIC, http://www.nationalgeographic.com/lostgospel/auth_evidence.html (last visited Nov. 1, 2010).

211. ROBINSON, *supra* note 190, at 53; DECONICK, *supra* note 190, at 3.

> They declare that Judas the traitor was thoroughly acquainted
> with these things, and that he alone, knowing the truth as no
> others did, accomplished the mystery of the betrayal; by him all
> things, both earthly and heavenly, were thus thrown into
> confusion. They produce a fabricated work to this effect, which
> they entitle *The Gospel of Judas*.[212]

The *Judas* tractate thus qualifies as an ancient document and, as such, is
excepted from hearsay objections.[213]

2. *Judas* as Witness

The credibility of the author of *Judas*, however, is an entirely different
matter. The author is essentially unknown, and there is no claim of
authorship in the document or elsewhere. "Contrast [the Gospel authors]
with what happened when the fanciful apocryphal gospels were written
much later. People chose the names of well-known and exemplary figures
to be their fictitious authors—Philip, Peter, Mary, James."[214]

At its earliest, the original content of the *Gospel of Judas* was likely
written in the mid-second century, perhaps 150 years after the events it
describes, compared to the canonical writers' contemporaneous
observations. *Judas* claims to be a "secret account of the revelation that
Jesus spoke in conversation with Judas Iscariot during a week three days
before he celebrated Passover."[215] It ends with Judas' interaction with the
high priests, where Judas "received some money and handed [Jesus] over to
them."[216] It is filled with purported conversations between Jesus and Judas
Iscariot to which there were no other witnesses.[217] In attempting to
determine the author's credibility as a witness, such a lack of corroborating
witnesses is particularly troubling. It is generally accepted that Judas

---

212. ROBINSON, *supra* note 190, at 54 (quoting IRENAEUS, REFUTATION OF ALL HERESIES,
at 1.31.1).

213. FED. R. EVID. 803(16).

214. STROBEL, *supra* note 11, at 27 (citing an interview with Craig L. Blomberg, Ph.D.).

215. *Gospel of Judas* 33 [hereinafter *Judas*] (unless otherwise indicated, page numbers
refer to tractate pages). The National Geographic translation incorporating the tractate pages
is available at http://www.nationalgeographic.com/lostgospel/_pdf/GospelofJudas.pdf (last
visited Nov. 1, 2010); *cf.* DECONICK, *supra* note 190, at 66-91 (DeConick's translation of
each page of the tractate shown by line).

216. *Judas*, *supra* note 215, at 58.

217. *E.g.*, *Judas*, *supra* note 215, at 35 ("Knowing that Judas was reflecting upon
something that was exalted, Jesus said to him, 'Step away from the others and I shall tell you
the mysteries of the kingdom. It is possible for you to reach it, but you will grieve a great
deal.'").

committed suicide immediately after he left Jesus.[218] Yet, there is no suggestion in the new document that Judas discussed these conversations with any confidant of his own, or that he shared his unique knowledge with anyone else before he took his own life. Nor is there a suggestion that he lived beyond the end of this "gospel."[219] The silence on these issues is deafening, particularly with no corroboration in any of the four canonical Gospels or in other sources, even for the events with the rest of the disciples that preface these conversations.

The comparison of *Judas* to the canonical texts supports their credibility while undermining the credibility of *Judas*. Greenleaf particularly noted the naturalness of the actions of the disciples and other characters in the Gospels, and of the authors' writings.[220] Descriptions of the disciples' questions and human concerns, their egos and attitudes, the response of the crowds—all ring true across the centuries to our own humanity. We can readily see and understand the occasional outbursts and doubts of the disciples, followed by moments of growing understanding and faith, particularly in the confirming appearances of the post-crucifixion Jesus. Yet the Judas of the newly translated gospel is pictured as being resented by the other disciples for being the only one with any intelligence or sense, while the remaining eleven dither in confusion and blasphemy.[221]

Analyzing *Judas* using either Greenleaf's five factors[222] or the *Crawford* reliability criteria[223] yields the same result. The testimony offered here bears none of the indicia of reliability required to be deemed credible. Those events that could have been witnessed are portrayed in a way that is contradictory to all known credible corroborated testimony. The people involved are barely described; there are insufficient details on which to base cross-examination of the testimony.

---

218. *Matthew* 27:5 (Complete Jewish Bible) ("Hurling the pieces of silver into the sanctuary, [Judas] left; then he went off and hanged himself."). *See also Acts* 1:18-20.

219. *Judas, supra* note 215, at 58.

220. TESTIMONY, *supra* note 5, § 46.

221. *Judas, supra* note 215, at 34. *But see* DECONICK, *supra* note 190, at 103-05. DeConick suggests that the *Judas* portrayal mirrors that found in *Mark*. *Id.* However, the humanity and growth in faith demonstrated by the disciples in the canonical Gospels is a far cry from the simplistic and uni-dimensional characterization in *Judas*.

222. Honesty, ability, number and consistency of testimony, conformity of testimony with experience, coincidence with collateral circumstances. TESTIMONY, *supra* note 5, § 29 (quoting STARKIE, *supra* note 57, at 480, 545; *see supra* Table 1.

223. Crawford v. Washington, 541 U.S. 36, 63 (2004) (discussing tests for reliability in, *inter alia*, Washington v. Crawford, 2001 Wash. App. LEXIS 1723 at *12 (citations omitted)). *See supra* notes 27, 168, 174.

While the evidence regarding the authors of the canonical Gospels rings credible in light of all these considerations, the story offered by the *Gospel of Judas* fails to ring at all. There are no corroborating witnesses to support its premise; there is no physical evidence or contemporaneous experience to endorse its claims.

3. Content and Context

While the Gospel testimonies are replete with particularized details that have withstood cross-examination for nearly two thousand years, there are few such details in *Judas* to be examined or corroborated. Because the Gnostic themes and beliefs were disparate from those of the early church, it is not surprising that documents such as those contained in the Nag Hammadi codices or the *Codex Tchacos* disappeared from sight. The *Judas* document in particular presents testimony contradicting that of the Gospels. And while the focus of the media has been primarily on the redemption of Judas' image, the focus of the canonical testimony has always been on the redemption of believers.

Judas "echoes the Platonic conviction that every person has his or her own star and that the fate of people is connected to their stars."[224] Judas is portrayed in an unusually positive light, the only one of the disciples to be taken into Jesus' confidence and the only one to understand the real reason Jesus was on the earth. The undertone throughout *Judas* lies in sharp contrast to the Gospel testimony, which was relied on by the early church, even before canonization. Of equal contrast is the view of the Gnostic sects regarding specialized esoteric knowledge as the road to salvation, rather than the sacrifice of Jesus. In fact, *Judas* ends with Judas handing Jesus to the priests, and does not include the crucifixion or the resurrection.[225] Only in the discussion between Judas and Jesus does Jesus allude to the act that will "sacrifice the man that clothes me."[226] Instead of the multiple, public, explicit discussions among Jesus and all of his disciples about the sacrifice Jesus is preparing to make for all humankind, relayed in the Gospels, *Judas* portrays one clandestine comment to a man whose image was in need of rehabilitation by the time the document was written, foretelling an act that would benefit only Jesus.

Even beyond its sanitization of the man himself, *Judas* is a decidedly Gnostic creation. As Jesus imparts his special knowledge to Judas, it is laced with a supernatural Gnostic tale of creation and the cosmos, stars and

---

224. KASSER ET AL., *supra* note 186, at 10.

225. *Judas*, *supra* note 215, at 58.

226. *Id.* at 56.

clouds, and the mysticism associated with those beliefs. Bart Ehrman describes the central themes of *Judas*:[227]

> For Gnostics, a person is saved not by having faith in Christ or by doing good works. Rather, a person is saved by knowing the truth—the truth about the world we live in, about who the true God is, and especially about who we ourselves are. In other words, this is largely self-knowledge: knowledge of where we came from, how we got here, and how we can return to our heavenly home.[228]

The god of the Gnostic vision diverges quickly from the God of Abraham. The Gnostic world portrayed in *Judas*

> is not the creation of the one true God. The god who made this world—the God of the Old Testament—is a secondary, inferior deity. He is not the God above all who is to be worshipped. Rather, he is to be avoided, by learning the truth about the ultimate divine realm, this evil material world, our entrapment here, and how we can escape.[229]

There is also disagreement as to the presence and form of Jesus here on earth:

> Some Gnostics taught that he was an aeon from the realm above . . . that he came from above only in the *appearance* of human flesh. . . . [A] phantasm who took on the appearance of flesh to teach those who were called (i.e., the Gnostics, who have the [divine] spark within) the secret truths they need for salvation. Other Gnostics taught that Jesus was a real man, but that he did not have a typical spark of divine within.[230]

The Gnostic Jesus would be touched with the spark for as long as he was on earth, in order to teach his lessons, then it would leave him when his earthly ministry was complete. *Judas* incorporates this attitude when it describes Jesus as not appearing "to his disciples as himself, but he was found among them as a child."[231] The majority of the content of *Judas* is

---

227. Bart D. Ehrman, *Christianity Turned on its Head: The Alternative Vision of the Gospel of Judas*, *in* KASSER ET AL., *supra* note 186, at 77-120.

228. *Id.* at 84.

229. Ehrman, *supra* note 227, at 86.

230. *Id.* at 87.

231. *Judas*, *supra* note 215, at 33.

similarly speculative, with no natural foundation or evidence of support. When viewed in total, whatever statements are made about the man Judas cannot be considered any more credible than the rest of the document.[232]

Further, the supernatural world portrayed in *Judas* can hardly be proved with natural evidence, and thus the context of these disparate documents is critically important in evaluating the veracity of each. The four canonical Gospels, written in the first century, "were written for, or addressed to, certain churches or individuals" in that place and time.[233] Their content was intended to address specific questions and needs of the immediate readers.[234] By contrast, *Judas* was written well into the second century by someone with an entirely different agenda from the testimony that met the needs and answered the questions of the early church. While the canonical Gospels provide first-person and first-generation accounts of the life, teachings, and sacrifice of Jesus, *Judas* appears to have been written solely to propagate the teachings of Gnosticism.[235] In the process (possibly in retaliation or response to what was becoming the official orthodoxy), Judas is portrayed not as the lone betrayer, but as the only disciple who understood Jesus. At the very least, Jesus is seen through a Gnostic lens. Judas from K'riot, the only non-Galilean, stands alone again, now in a place of honor rather than infamy.[236]

After Peter's attestation at Caesarea Philippi that Jesus was the Messiah,[237] Jesus and his *talmidim* traveled from the northern heights (Golan) to Jerusalem. Quite unlike the lone witness portrayed in *Judas*, all twelve were provided an insight into what lay ahead for Jesus. On at least three occasions, Jesus shared with them that he would be betrayed, condemned, and killed, but ultimately resurrected.[238] Unlike the surreptitious, solo performance just for Judas, there were at least twelve

---

232. *See* FED. R. EVID. 106 (informally known as the rule of completeness).

233. HENRY M. HALLEY, HALLEY'S BIBLE HANDBOOK 458 (23d ed. 1962).

234. *See, e.g., Luke* 1:1-4; NICKLE, *supra* note 80, at 7-9; FEE & STUART, *supra* note 151, at 128-31.

235. DECONICK, *supra* note 190, at 17-42.

236. *But see* DECONICK, *supra* note 190, at 46-47. DeConick questions National Geographic's initial translation: "I began to become concerned with their English translation of several passages of the Coptic, translations that appeared to me not only faulty, but faulty in a certain way. . . . [M]y translation of the Gospel suggested that Judas was as evil as ever . . ." *Id.*

237. *Matthew* 16:13-20; *Mark* 8:27-30; *Luke* 9:18-20.

238. The three discussions are each reported in all three synoptic Gospels: (1) *Matthew* 16:21-23; *Mark* 8:31-33; *Luke* 9:21, 22; (2) *Matthew* 17:22, 23; *Mark* 9:30-32; *Luke* 9:43-45; (3) *Matthew* 20:17-19; *Mark* 10:32-34; *Luke* 18:31-34.

witnesses to these lessons. More important, Jesus' purpose in undergoing these trials was far different from that portrayed in *Judas*. Rather than undergoing trials to give glory to God,[239] the Jesus described in the *Gospel of Judas* is using the crucifixion as a means to his own end, merely to "sacrifice the man that clothes me."[240]

Fee and Stuart focus the study of any narrative at three levels—first, through the individuals' stories or narratives, then as the story of "God's redeeming a people for his name," and, finally, in the big picture or "meta-narrative" of God's universal redemptive story.[241] In evaluating witness credibility, this perspective aids in comparison of context and content between the canonical Gospels and the *Gospel of Judas*. As discussed *supra* in Section II.B.2, the individual testimonies of Matthew, Mark, Luke, and John complement each other, being substantially similar in tone and content, yet containing the minor discrepancies that would be expected among witnesses to the same events, particularly when writing to different audiences with different purposes. In that respect, they stand in stark contrast to *Judas*. While the Gospels show a very human, multi-dimensional group of men with all their personalities, foibles, and reactions to the events during Jesus' ministry, *Judas* portrays a monolithic bloc of disciples totally unaware of why they devoted three years of their lives trying to emulate their teacher. The focus of *Judas* is only incidentally on Jesus, and much more on Judas and the Gnostic cosmos.

In the same way, in *Judas* there is no redemption of a people. Instead of the sacrifice of Jesus for the salvation of "whosoever [will] believe,"[242] Jew and Gentile alike, Judas' handing over merely allows Jesus to be released from his human shell. Others who also hold the Gnostic divine spark within them may ultimately join him in the heavens, but his presence or absence from this world will have no impact on anyone else's ultimate fate. *Judas* posits that the "creator of this world is not the one true God; this world is an evil place to be escaped; Christ is not the son of the creator; salvation comes not through the death and resurrection of Jesus, but through the revelation of secret knowledge that he provides."[243] *Judas* asserts an agenda

---

239. *John* 17:1.

240. *Judas*, *supra* note 215, at 56.

241. FEE & STUART, *supra* note 151, at 90-91.

242. *John* 3:15.

243. Ehrman, *supra* note 219, at 102.

with no link to history or community; the Gospels proffer testimony of promise fulfilled.[244]

IV. CONCLUSION

More than a century and a half has passed since Greenleaf first challenged his legal colleagues to consider the testimony of the first century evangelists, to "try their veracity by the ordinary tests of truth, admitted in human tribunals."[245] He demonstrated the credibility of the canonical Gospels, relying on evidentiary standards that remain essentially unchanged today, "for it is by such evidence alone that our rights are determined, in the civil tribunals; and on no other evidence do they proceed, even in capital cases."[246] The standards have not changed, and indeed the corroborating evidence is even stronger today than when Greenleaf completed his analysis. The conclusion, therefore, remains the same as well. Moreover, the strength of the evidentiary legal standard and its support for the credibility of the testimony allows today's objective juror to take the final step over the natural/supernatural wall to view all of the evidence.

Faced with such cogent evidence, those who wish to avoid God—or any hint of the sacred—will struggle to find an alternative explanation, while offering not a shred of the evidence they demand from others. For some, even extra-terrestrial aliens are accepted more readily than the God portrayed in the Gospels.[247] A naturalist may suggest:

---

244. Complete Jewish Bible, *supra* note 93, at xliii-xlvii (listing *Tanakh* prophesies fulfilled by Jesus).

245. TESTIMONY, *supra* note 5, § 35.

246. *Id.* § 41.

247. EXPELLED: NO INTELLIGENCE ALLOWED (Rampant Films 2008). In an interview with Ben Stein, atheist professor and author Richard Dawkins stated:

[I]t could be that at some earlier time somewhere in the universe a civilization evolved, by probably some kind of Darwinian means, to a very very high level of technology, and designed a form of life that they seeded onto perhaps this planet. That is a possibility, and an intriguing possibility, and I suppose it's possible that you might find evidence for that if you look at the details of bio-chemistry, molecular biology, you might find a signature of some sort of designer . . . and that designer could well be a higher intelligence from elsewhere in the universe.

Id. See also Ancient Aliens Theory, HISTORY.COM, http://www.history.com/shows/ancient-aliens/articles/ancient-alien-theory (last visited July 30, 2010); *Evidence of Ancient Aliens?*, HISTORY.COM, http://www.history.com/shows/ancient-aliens/articles/evidence-of-ancient-aliens (last visited May 1, 2010); George Sassoon & Rodney Dale, *The Manna Machine*, http://www.fernhouse.com/book-pages/mannamachine.html (last visited May 1, 2010).

> The reason some people switch to faith in these areas [of human nature, consciousness, freedom, and the like] is that they may not like the answers science provides, and they find the answers of faith more reassuring. So, here's the question: do you want the empirical truth that's backed up by evidence . . . ?[248]

But this is precisely the question the naturalist must answer: Do you want the empirical truth that is backed up by the evidence of the Gospels? If the evidence is credible by a legal standard, does it not lead to the truth?[249]

"There may be other values, and at the end of the day they may outweigh the gains to factual accuracy that may be at play in some policy choice, but it is our job to ensure that the primacy of facts is never neglected."[250] Thus, the primacy of the evidentiary analysis, i.e., the search for the facts, should not be neglected simply because the analysis takes the inquirer to the other side of the wall. "Let the witnesses be compared with themselves, with each other, and with surrounding facts and circumstances; and let their testimony be sifted, as if it were given in a court of justice, on the side of the adverse party, the witness being subjected to a rigorous cross-examination."[251] Such rigor should also be applied to conflicting theories, especially for those who would ignore the existence of credible evidence while at the same time holding onto *Da Vinci* conspiracy theories without any factual basis whatsoever. Religion cannot be used to impugn credibility,[252]

> [b]ut the Christian writer seems, by the usual course of the argument, to have been deprived of the common presumption of charity in his favor; and reversing the ordinary rule of administering justice in human tribunals, his testimony is unjustly presumed to be false, until it is proved to be true. This treatment, moreover, has been applied to them all in a body; and, without due regard to the fact, that, being independent historians, writing at different periods, they are entitled to the support of each other: they have been treated, in the argument, almost as if the New Testament were the entire production, at once, of a

---

248. CENTER FOR NATURALISM, *supra* note 15.

249. FED. R. EVID. 102 (stating that the Rules of Evidence "shall be construed . . . to the end that the truth may be ascertained . . . .").

250. Allen, *supra* note 16, at 16.

251. TESTIMONY, *supra* note 5, § 42.

252. FED. R. EVID. 610.

body of men, conspiring by a joint fabrication, to impose a false religion upon the world.[253]

This may be the greatest irony of the naturalistic inquiry. As Greenleaf's evidentiary analysis continues to demonstrate, facts and secular evidence exist on the supernatural side of the wall, proving credible the testimony of the Gospels. Yet, because naturalism expressly eliminates consideration of the "supernatural,"[254] its questions encompass only half an inquiry; its answers are founded on only half the data. Its "self-imposed convention"[255] can never yield a complete answer because it does not allow a crossing of the wall to find factual, natural evidence on the other side. As demonstrated by Greenleaf's analytical construct, and in complete contrast to *Judas*, the testimony of the life, times, and message of Jesus presented by Matthew, Mark, Luke, and John is credible "evidence to the end that the truth may be ascertained,"[256] despite the testimony's being found in sacred text.

And so we consider now the testimonies from a lawyer's perspective, as evidence presented to a jury, weighing "the veracity of the witnesses and the credibility of their narratives."[257] Examine the evidence, draw the inferences, make the deductions, reach the conclusions. Certainly, some readers of this Article will never be able to lay aside their preconceptions or to view the testimony as objective jurors. Some, having long since accepted the Gospels in faith, will not rely on legal argument to convince them of the credibility of the testimony. But those who have read this Article to the end, with an open and objective mind, surely now realize that the evidence presented by the canonical Gospels is credible even under current rules of legal evidence; that the testimony presented there has not been successfully challenged or impeached in nearly 2000 years; and, finally, that the testimony credibly demonstrates that the Jesus who walked those pages, and worked miracles, and claimed to be the Son of the living God,[258]—

---

253. TESTIMONY, *supra* note 5, § 28.

254. *See Worldview Naturalism: A Status Report*, NATURALISM.ORG, http://naturalism.org/landscape.htm (last visited October 18, 2010).

255. Kitzmiller v. Dover Area Sch. Dist., 400 F. Supp. 2d 707, 735 (M.D. Pa. 2005) (noting the so-called "scientific method" is based on the "self-imposed convention" of solely natural observation).

256. FED. R. EVID. 102.

257. TESTIMONY, *supra* note 5, § 48.

258. *See, e.g., John* 10:22-30; *John* 12:20-26; *John* 17:1-5.

indeed, the Messiah of prophecy[259]—is, in fact, the very man he is portrayed to be in the recorded testimony of the four Gospels.

The Rules of Evidence create a framework to determine the truth, and Greenleaf's analytic construct still serves the rules in that search. We should not be afraid of where the truth leads us, however strange, disconcerting, or challenging it may be. Now, as in Greenleaf's day, as in the days of the testimony, "If you obey what I say, then you are really my *talmidim*, you will know the truth, and the truth will set you free."[260]

---

259. *See, e.g., John* 4:24-26. This "answers everyone who questions whether Yeshua proclaimed his own Messiahship. The declaration, 'I am,' echoes *Adonai's* self-revelation, 'I am who I am' (*Exodus* 3:14). Yeshua says this 'I am' nine times in [John's] Gospel (here; 6:20; 8:24, 28, 58; 13:9; 18:5, 6, 8), implying a claim even greater than being the Messiah." STERN, *supra* note 13, at 168.

260. *John* 8:31-32 (Complete Jewish Bible) (quoting Jesus in the temple in Jerusalem, speaking with those who had come to believe in Him).

Notes

Notes to Chapter 1

1. B. Cardozo, *Law and Literature*, in *Essays on Jurisprudence from the Colum. L. Rev.* 313 (1963).

2. L. Fuller, *The Problems of Jurisprudence passim* (1949). See also Fuller, *The Case of the Speluncean Explorers*, 62 *Harv. L. Rev.* 616 (1949).

3. The *Code* was adopted by the House of Delegates of the ABA on August 12, 1969, to become effective on January 1, 1970; it was amended on February 24, 1970. The *Code* enlarges upon and officially replaces the ABA's *Canons of Professional Ethics*, adopted in 1908 and subsequently amended.

4. ABA *Code of Professional Responsibility* EC 1-5.

5. M. L. Schwartz, *Law Schools and Ethics, Chronicle of Higher Education*, Dec. 9, 1974, at 20; *cf.* ABA *Canons of Professional Ethics* No. 15: The attorney "must obey his own conscience and not that of his client" (*see also* No. 18). But what value system is to inform the attorney's conscience? "[N]o client has a right to demand that his counsel shall be illiberal, or that he do anything therein repugnant to his own sense of honor and propriety" (No. 24; *cf.* No. 44). "Illiberal" by what criterion? "Honor and "Propriety" by whose definition?

6. ABA *Code of Professional Responsibility* Preamble. See also ABA *Canons* No. 32.

7. *Uniform Commercial Code* § 1-205, Comment 6.

8. Trist v. Child, 88 U.S. (21 Wall.) 441 (1874) (Swayne, J.).

9. A. Solzhenitsyn, *The Gulag Archipelago 1918-1956* pt. 1 (1974); cf. *A Solzhenitsyn: Critical Essays and Documentary Materials* (J. B. Dunlop, R. Haugh & A. Klimoff ed. 1973).

10. *E.g.*, *International Commission of Jurists, Justice Enslaved: A Collection of Documents on the Abuse of Justice for Political Ends* (1955).

11. See *V. I. Lenin et al.*, *Soviet Legal Philosophy passim* (20th Century Legal Philosophy Ser. Vol. 5, 1951); *cf. R. David & J. Brierley, Major Legal Systems in the World Today* 157-58 (1968).

12. See. *J. W. Montgomery, The Shape of the Past* 74, 80, 217 (1963).

13. *Cf. J. Fletcher & J. W. Montgomery, Situation Ethics: True or False* 79, 82, 83 (1972).

14. *W. L. Burdick, The Bench and Bar of Other Lands* 422 (1939).

15. *E.g.*, George A. Finch and Professor Edwin Borchard: 41 *Am. J. Int'l L.* 20, 107, 334 (1947); *cf. R. Wormser, The Story of the Law* 557 (rev. ed. 1962).

16. R. Jackson, *Closing Address in the Nuremberg Trial*, in 19 *Proceedings in the Trial of the Major War Criminals Before the International Military Tribunal* 397 (1948). For valuable bibliographical references on the Nuremberg trial, see *W. Bishop, International Law* 996, 1016-18 (3d ed., 1971).

17. H.L.A. Hart, *Philosophy of Law, Problems of*, in 6 *Encyclopedia of Philosophy* 264, 270 (P. Edwards ed. 1967).

18. L.R. 3 H.L. 330 (1868).

19. 2 Ex. D. 1 (1876).

20. A.W.B. Simpson, *The "Ratio Decidendi" of a Case and the Doctrine of Binding Precedent*, in *Oxford Essays in Jurisprudence (First Ser.)* 148, 175 (2nd ed. A. G. Guest 1968).

21. Leavitt v. Morrow, 6 Ohio St. 71, 67 Am. Dec. 334 (1856).

22. A. Corbin, *Cases on the Law of Contracts* 916 (3d ed. 1947).

23. *Cf. A.V. Dicey, Law & Public Opinion in England During the 19th Century* 375-82 (2d ed. 1914, reissued 1962), and Lord Justice James' remarks on the oppressive character of older chancery pleadings: Davy v. Garrett, 38 L.T.R. (m.s.) 81 (1878).

24. *J. A. Duncan, The Strangest Cases on Record* 183-84 (1940); *cf. B. Warée, Curiosités judiciaires* 385-98 (1859).

25. *A Volansky, Essai d'une définition expressive du Droit basée sur l'idée de bonne foi* (1930).

26. See *Uniform Commercial Code* §§ 1-203; 2-209, Comment 2; 2-305, Comment 6; 2-306, Comment 1; 2-309, Comment 5; etc.

27. *Lord Radcliffe, The Law & Its Compass: 1960 Rosenthal Lectures, Northwestern University School of Law* 33, 57 (1961).

28. *H.L.A. Hart, The Concept of Law* 105-106 (1965); *cf. Symposium: The Philosophy of H.L.A. Hart*, in 35 *U. Chi. L. Rev.* 1 (1967); *Philosophies du droit anglaises et américaines*, in 15 *Archives de Philosophie du Droit* 113, 179 (1970); and R. Sartorius, *Hart's Concept of Law*, in *More Essays in Legal Philosophy* 131 (R. Summers Ed. 1971).

29. Lecture delivered by Hans Kelsen at the University of California, Nov. 20, 1962 (tape at Boalt Hall Library; *cf.* R. G. Decker, *The Secularization of Anglo-American Law: 1800-1970*, in 49 *Thought* 280, 292-93, 297 (1974); A. S. de Bustamante ye Montoro, *Kelsenism*, in *Interpretations of Modern Legal Philosophies: Essays in Honor of Roscoe Pound* 43 (P. Sayre ed. 1947); and M. P. Golding, *Kelsen and the Concept of 'Legal System'*, in *More Essays in Legal Philosophy* 69 (R. Summers Ed. 1971).

30. See *J. W. Montgomery, Where is History Going?* 15-36 (1969).

31. W. Allen, *My Philosophy*, in *The New Yorker*, Dec. 27, 1969, at 25.

32. L. Wittgenstein, *Tractatus Logico-Philosophicus* §§6.41-6.421.

33. Wittgenstein, *Lecture on Ethics*, 74 *Phil. Rev.* 3, 7 (1965).

34. *Cf. I. T. Ramsey, Religious Language passim* (1957).

35. *J.-J. Rousseau, Contrat social*, Bk. 2, ch. 7.

36. "The revival of natural-law doctrines is one of the most interesting features of current legal thought"—M. P. Golding, *Philosophy of Law, History of*, in 6 *Encyclopedia of Philosophy* 254, 263 (P. Edwards ed. 1967). *Cf. J. Charmont, La Renaissance du Droit naturel* (2d ed. 1927); *C. G. Haines, The Revival of Natural Law Concepts* (Harv. Studies in Juris. Vol. 4, reprint ed. 1965); *J. Cogley, R. M. Hutchins et al., Natural Law and Modern Society* (1966); *F. Castberg, La Philosophie du Droit* (1970). For a detailed expression of traditional Natural Law theory, see *Th. Jouffroy, Cours de droit naturel* (5th ed. 1876).

37. M. T. Cicero, *De Legibus* bk. 2, ch. 4.

38. *Cf. A. d'Entrèves, Natural Law* 22 (2d ed. 1970).

39. C. J. Friedrich, *The Philosophy of Law in Historical Perspective* 22 (2d ed. 1963).

40. A useful list is provided in *C. S. Lewis, The Abolition of Man* 51 (1947).

41. *Cf.* J. W. Montgomery, *How to Decide the Birth Control Question*, in *Birth Control and the Christian* 575 (W. Spitzer & C. Saylor ed. 1969).

42. L. H. Perkins, *Natural Law in Contemporary Analytic Philosophy*, 17 *Am. J. Juris.* 111, 118 (1972).

43. *Cf. G. Del Vecchio's* argument that veracity constitutes a juridical obligation: *La Justice—La Vérité: Essais de philosophie juridique et morale* 173, 195, 231 (1955).

44. Personal observation of the author.

45. *C. G. Haines, supra* note 36, at vii.

46. See *T. E. Holland, The Elements of Jurisprudence* 33 (13th ed. 1924); and *cf. E. Zeller, Outlines of the History of Greek Philosophy* 209, 266 (13th ed. W. Nestle 1931), and his *Stoics, Epicureans, and Sceptics* (1870).

47. *Acts* 17:18-19, 22-23, 30-31. It is noteworthy that in v. 28 Paul quotes Stoic philosophical poetry; the reference is almost certainly to Cleanthes' "Hymn to Zeus"—text in *Essential Works of Stoicism* 51 (M. Hadas ed. 1965).

48. *John* 1:17.

49. *Cf. Acts* 17:6, where the early preachers of the gospel are referred to by their opponents as "these who have turned the world upside down."

50. *Hebrews* 4:15.

51. *R. David & J. Brierley, supra* note 11, at 386: ". . . Muslim jurists and theologians have built up a complete and detailed law on the basis of divine revelation [the Koran]—the law of an ideal society which one day will be established in a world entirely subject to Islamic religion."

52. See J. W. Montgomery, *The Apologetic Approach of Muhammad Ali and Its Implications for Christian Apologetics*, 51 *Muslim World* 111 (1961); *cf. Corrigendum* in July, 1961 *Muslim World.*

53. For other important examples, together with detailed discussion of the arguments briefly mentioned here, see *J. W. Montgomery, Jurisprudence: A Book of Readings passim* (1974).

54. Greenleaf's Seminal Essay is included as Appendix to the present work, with the typographical errors of the earlier editions now corrected.

55. These works can be obtained from, respectively, Tyndale Press, 39 Bedford Sq., London, Eng. and Inter-Versity Press, Downers Grove, Ill.

56. *J. W. Montgomery, History & Christianity* (1970); Montgomery, *Legal Reasoning & Christian*

Apologetics, Christianity Today, Feb. 14, 1975.

57. *2 Peter* 1:16.

58. The classic Formulation of *T. Starkie*: 1 *Law of Evidence* 478 (2d ed. 1833); *cf. Wigmore, Treatise on Evidence* § 2497. See also *J. Gambier, Moral Evidence* (3d ed. 1824), and *A. Bucknill, The Nature of Evidence* (1953).

59. Commonwealth v. Webster, 59 Mass. (5 Cush.) 295, 52 Am. Dec. 711 (1850). *Cf. L. W. Levy, The Law of the Commonwealth and Chief Justice Shaw* 218-28 (1957, reprinted 1967).

60. *Acts* 1:1-3

61. *Acts* 17:26; *Galatians* 3:28.

62. *Thomas Mann, The Tables of the Law* 61-62 (H. T. Lowe-Porter transl. 1945).

63. *Id.* at 62-63.

64. See *J. W. Montgomery, The Law's Third Use*, in *The Suicide of Christian Theology* 423 (1970).

65. *Galatians* 3:24. The Greek word translated "Schoolmaster" in the King James Version (παιδαγωγός: *paedagogos*) referred not to the teacher himself but to the slave whose responsibility it was to take the pupil to the teacher.

66. *Matthew* 5:17 *ff.*

67. *James* 2:10; *cf. Matthew* 5:48.

68. *Romans* 3:23.

69. *John* 3:16; *Romans* 5:6-8; 6:23; *Ephesians* 2:8-9.

70. *M. Luther, In Epistolam S. Pauli and Galatas commentarius* (1531), in 40 *WA* (the standard, critical *Weimarer Ausgabe* of the Reformer's writings) pt. 1 at 482. For an English transl. of Luther's great Galatians Commentary, see P. S. Watson's rev. (1956) of the Middleton ed. (cited passage at 299); see also *M. Luther, Selections* 141 (J. Dillenberger ed. 1961). *Cf. C. F. W. Walther, The Proper Distinction Between Law and Gospel passim* (1928).

71. *P. Calamandrei, Eulogy of Judges* 101 (1942).

72. [*J. A. Foote*], *"Pie-Powder," Being Dust from the Law Courts, Collected and Recollected on the Western Circuit by a Circuit Tramp* 213-14 (1911, reprinted 1967).

73. *J. C. Gray, The Nature and Sources of the Law* 84 (2d ed. R. Gray 1921, reprinted 1963).

74. *Luke* 12:2-3.

75. See *K. Heim, Jesus the World's Perfecter: The Atonement and the Renewal of the World* pt. 3 (1959); *J. P. Martin, The Last Judgment* (1963); and especially *M. Barth, Acquittal by Resurrection*, ch. 4 (1964).

76. 1 *John* 2:1; *Romans* 14:10-12; *Philippians* 2:10.

77. Fortunately, our Founding Fathers (with the prominent exception of Jefferson) did not consciously attempt to cut themselves off from their revelational roots (see *E. S. Corwin, The "Higher Law" Background of American Constitutional Law* [1955]). In developing their views of "inalienable rights" and social contract they followed not the deistic sentimentalist Rousseau but John Locke—whose Christian beliefs were so firm that he wrote an apologetic on *The Reasonableness of Christianity* (cf. *C. Becker, The Declaration of Independence: A Study in the History of Ideas* (rev. ed. 1942]). Jefferson's antipathy to Blackstone may well relate not only to the latter's political but also to his religious conservatism; see *J. S. Waterman, Thomas Jefferson and Blackstone's Commentaries*, in *Essays in the History of Early American Law* 451, 472-73 (D. H. Flaherty ed. 1969).

78. Cf. *Radical Lawyers: Their Role in the Movement and in the Courts* (J. Black ed. 1971).

79. 2 *Thessalonians* 2:8.

80. *Luke* 15:16 ff.

Notes to Chapter 2

1. *Principalities and Powers: The World of the*

Occult (Minneapolis: Bethany Fellowship, Inc., 1973).
This book is now available in a paperback edition.

2. Harvard University Press, 1929.

3. Groningen, 1953, pp. 408-415.

4. Vol. I, chap. xvii.

5. *City of God*, bk. XIX, chap. vi.

6. "Quod vero confession cruciatibus extorquenda non est," Caus. XV, qu. 6, can. 1.

7. *Superstition and Force: Essays on the Wager of Law—the Wager of Battle—the Ordeal—Torture*, 2d ed. (New York: Greenwood Press reprint, 1968). p. 370.

8. Trans. Simpson (Rothman Reprints, 1968), p. 9.

9. *De praestigiis daemonum* (1953).

10. *The Discoverie of Witchcraft* (1584).

11. See Julio Caro Baroja, *The World of the Witches*, trans. Glendinning (Chicago: University of Chicago Press, 1964), chap. xiv.

12. See also Roland Villeneuve, *Les proces de sorcellerie* (Verviers, Belgium: Marabout, 1974), chap. ix.

13. H. B. Clark, ed., *Biblical Law* (2d ed., 1944), para. 70; cf. Montgomery, *Jurisprudence: A Book of Readings* (Washington, D.C.: Lerner Law Books, 1974).

14. See William Holdsworth, *The History of English Law*, 3d ed., I, 508-516.

15. Cf. Sir Charles Oman, *The Sixteenth Century* (Dutton, 1937), chap. xii.

16. P. 373; cf. John M. Taylor, *The Witchcraft Delusion in Colonial Connecticut* (1908), pp. 27-28.

17. Henry Charles Lea, *Materials Toward a History of Witchcraft*, I, 244.

18. *Ibid.*, II, 901-902.

19. *Witchcraft in England* (New York: Scribner, 1947), p. 62; cf. her *Mirror of Witchcraft* (London:

Chatto & Windus, 1957), pp. 181ff.

20. *Dictionary of American Biography*, VII, 598, *in loco*; cf. C. W. Upham, *Salem Witchcraft* (1867), Vol. II.

21. See Max Farrand's edition of the *Body of Liberties* (1929), p. 50, and cf. Max Radin, *Handbook of Anglo-American Legal History* (1936), para. 50.

22. Paris, 1580, bk. IV, chap. v.

23. See my debate with Joseph Fletcher: *Situation Ethics: True or False* (Minneapolis: Bethany Fellowship, Inc., 1972).

24. Lea, *op. cit.*, I, 244.

25. Bremen, 1661.

26. Lea, *op. cit.*, bk. II, 805.

Notes to Appendix

1. This article examines the testimony of the evangelists by the rules of evidence administered in courts of justice. It is here republished, with corrections, from the *Soney & Sage* (Newark, N.J.) edition of 1903. The late author, a professor of law in Harvard University, also authored *Treatise on the Law of Evidence*.

2. Nov. Org. 1. 68. "Ut non alius fere sit aditus ad regnum hominis, quod fundatur in scientiis, quam ad regnum coelorum in quod, nisi sub persona infantis, intrare non datur."

3. Bishop Wilson's Evidences, p. 38.

4. See Dr. Hopkins's Lowell Lectures, particularly Lec. 2. Bp. Wilson's Evidences of Christianity, Vol. i. pp. 45-61. Horne's Introduction, Vol. i. pp. 1-39. Mr. Horne having cited all the best English writers on this subject, it is sufficient to refer to his work alone.

5. Hopkins's Lowell Lect., p. 48.

6. It has been well remarked, that, if we regard man as in a state of innocence, we should naturally expect that God would hold communications with him;

that if we regard him as guilty, and as having lost the knowledge and moral image of God, such a communication would be absolutely necessary, if man was to be restored. Dr. Hopkins's Lowell Lect., p. 62.

7. The argument here briefly sketched is stated more at large, and with great clearness and force, in an essay entitled "The Philosophy of the Plan of Salvation," pp. 13-107.

8. See Professor Stuart's Critical History and Defense of the Old Testament Canon, where this is abundantly proved.

9. Per *Tindal*, Ch. J., in the case of Bishop of Meath *v.* Marquis of Winchester, 3 Bing. N.C. 183, 200, 201. "It is when documents are found in other than their proper places of deposit," observed the Chief Justice, "that the investigation commences, whether it was reasonable and natural, under the circumstances of the particular case, to expect that they should have been in the place where they are actually found; for it is obvious, that, while there can be only one place of deposit strictly and absolutely proper, there may be many and various, that are reasonable and probable, though differing in degree, some being more so, some less; and in these cases the proposition to be determined is, whether the actual custody is so reasonably and probably accounted for, that it impresses the mind with the conviction that the instrument found in such custody must be genuine." See the cases cited in Greenl. on Ev. § 142; see also 1 Stark. on Ev. pp. 332-335. 381-386; Croughton *v.* Blake, 12 Mees, & W. 205, 208; Doe *v.* Phillips, 10 Jur. 34. It is this defect, namely, that they do not come from the proper or natural repository, which shows the fabulous character of many pretended revelations, from the Gospel of the Infancy to the Book of Mormon.

10. 1 Greenl. on Ev. 34, 142, 570.

11. Morewood *v.* Wood, 14 East, 329, n., per Lord *Kenyon*; Weeks *v.* Sparke, 1 M. & S. 686; Berkeley Peerage Case, 4 Campb. 416, per *Mansfield*, Ch. J.; see 1 Greenl. on Ev. § 128.

12. 1 Stark, on Ev. pp. 195, 230; 2 Greenl. on Ev. § 483.

13. The arguments for the genuineness and authenticity of the books of the Holy Scriptures are briefly, yet very fully stated, and almost all the writers of authority are referred to by Mr. Horne, in his Introduction to the Study of the Holy Scriptures, vol. i., *passim.* The same subject is discussed in a more popular manner in the Lectures of Bishop Wilson, and of Bishop Sumner of Chester, on the Evidences of Christianity; and, in America, the same question, as it relates to the Gospels, has been argued by Bishop McIlvaine, in his Lectures.

14. See the case of the Slane Peerage, 5 Clark & F. 24. See also the case of the Fitzwalter Peerage, 10 Id. 948.

15. Matt. ix. 10; Mark ii. 14, 15; Luke v. 29.

16. The authorities on this subject are collected in Horne's Introduction vol. iv. pp. 234-238, part 2, chap. ii. sec. 2.

17. See Horne's Introduction, vol. iv. pp. 229-232.

18. See Campbell on the Four Gospels, vol. iii. pp. 35, 36; Preface to St. Matthew's Gospel, § 22, 23.

19. See Gibbon's Rome, vol. i. ch. vi. and vol. iii. ch. xvii. and authorities there citied. Cod. Theod. Lib. xi. tit. 1-28, with the notes of Gothofred. Gibbon treats particularly of the revenues of a latter period than our Saviour's time; but the general course of proceeding, in the levy and collection of taxes, is not known to have been changed since the beginning of the empire.

20. Acts xii. 12, 25; xiii. 5, 13; and xv. 36-41; 2 Tim. iv. 11; Phil. 24; Col. iv. 10; 1 Pet. v. 13.

21. Horne's Introduction, vol. ix. pp. 252, 253.

22. Mark vii. 2, 11; and ix. 43, and elsewhere.

23. Mr. Norton has conclusively disposed of this objection, in his Evidences of the Genuineness of the Gospels, vol. i. Additional Notes, sec. 2, pp. cxv-cxxxii.

24. Compare Mark x. 46, and xiv. 69, and iv. 35, and i. 35, and ix. 28, with Matthew's narrative of the same events.

25. See Horne's Introd. vol. iv. pp. 252-259.

26. Acts xvi. 10, 11.

27. Col. iv. 14. Luke, the beloved physician.

28. Luke v. 12; Matt. viii. 2; Mark i. 40.

29. Luke vi. 6; Matt. xii. 10; Mark iii. 1.

30. Luke viii. 55; Matt. ix. 25; Mark v. 42.

31. Luke vi. 13.

32. Luke xxii. 44, 45, 51.

33. See Horne's Introd. vol. iv. pp. 260-272, where references may be found to earlier writers.

34. See Lardner's Works, 8vo. vol. vi. pp. 138, 139; 4to. vol. iii. pp. 203, 204; and other authors, cited in Horne's Introd. vol. i. p. 267.

35. 2 Phill. on Ev. p. 95 (9th edition).

36. When Abbot, Archbishop of Canterbury, in shooting a dear with a cross-bow, in Bramsil park, accidentally killed the keeper, King James I, by a letter dated Oct. 3, 1621, requested the Lord Keeper, the Lord Chief Justice, and others, to inquire into the circumstances and consider the case and "the scandal that may have risen thereupon," and to certify the King what it may amount to. Could there be any reasonable doubt of their report of the facts, thus ascertained? See Spelman's Posthumous Works, p. 121.

37. The case of the ill-fated steamer President furnishes an example of this sort of inquiry. This vessel, it is well known, sailed from New York for London in the month of March, 1841, having on board many passengers, some of whom were highly connected. The ship was soon overtaken by a storm, after which she was never heard of. A few months afterwards a solemn inquiry was instituted by three gentlemen of respectability, one of whom was a British admiral, another was agent for the underwriters at Lloyd's, and the other a government packet agent, concerning the time, circumstances and causes of that disaster; the result of which was communicated to the public, under their hands. This document received universal confidence, and no further inquiry was made.

38. Mark. i. 20.

39. John xix. 26, 27.

40. John xiii. 23.

41. Matt. xxvii. 55, 56; Mark xv. 40, 41.

42. John xviii. 15, 16.

43. Luke viii. 51; Matt. xvii. 1, and xxvi. 37.

44. This account is abridged from Horne's Introd. vol. iv. pp. 286-288.

45. Horne's Introd. vol. iv. p. 289, and authors there cited.

46. See, among others, John i. 38, 41, and ii. 6, 13, and iv. 9, and xi. 55.

47. See Horne's Introd. vol. iv. pp. 297, 298.

48. See Gambier's Guide to the Study of Moral Evidence, p. 121.

49. 1 Stark. on Ev. pp. 514, 577; 1 Greenl. on Ev. §§ 1, 2; Willis on Circumstantial Ev. p. 2; Whately's Logic, b. iv. ch. iii. §1.

50. See 1 Stark. on Ev. pp. 16, 480, 521.

51. This subject has been treated by Dr. Chalmers, in his Evidences of the Christian Revelation, chapter iii. The following extract from his observations will not be unacceptable to the reader. "In other cases, when we compare the narratives of contemporary historians, it is not expected that all the circumstances alluded to by one will be taken notice of by the rest; and it often happens that an event or a custom is admitted upon the faith of a single historian; and the silence of all other writers is not suffered to attach suspicion or discredit to his testimony. It is an allowed principle, that a scrupulous resemblance betwixt two histories is very far from necessary to their being held consistent with one another. And what is more, it sometimes happens that, with contemporary historians, there may be an apparent contradiction, and the credit of both parties remain as entire and unsuspicious as before. Posterity is, in these cases, disposed to make the most liberal allowances. Instead of calling it a contradiction, they often call it a difficulty. They are sensible that, in many instances a seeming variety of statement has, upon a more extensive knowledge of ancient history, admitted of a perfect reconciliation. Instead, then, of referring the difficulty in question to the inaccuracy or bad faith of any of the parties, they, with more justness and more modesty, refer it to their own ignorance, and to that obscurity which necessarily hangs over the history

of every remote age. These principles are suffered to have great influence in every secular investigation; but so soon as, instead of a secular, it becomes a sacred investigation, every ordinary principle is abandoned, and the suspicion annexed to the teachers of religion is carried to the dereliction of all that candor and liberality with which every other document of antiquity is judged of and appreciated. How does it happen that the authority of Josephus should be acquiesced in as a first principle, while every step, in the narrative of the evangelists, must have foreign testimony to confirm and support it? How comes it, that the silence of Josephus should be construed into an impeachment of the testimony of the evangelists, while it is never admitted, for a single moment, that the silence of the evangelists, can impart the slightest blemish to the testimony of Josephus? How comes it, that the supposition of two Philips in one family should throw a damp of scepticism over the Gospel narrative, while the only circumstance which renders that supposition necessary is the single testimony of Josephus; in which very testimony it is necessarily implied that there are two Herods in that same family? How comes it, that the evangelists, with as much internal, and a vast deal more of external evidence in their favor, should be made to stand before Josephus, like so many prisoners at the bar of justice? In any other case, we are convinced that this would be looked upon as *rough handling*. But we are not sorry for it. It has given more triumph and confidence to the argument. And it is no small addition to our faith, that its first teachers have survived an examination, which, in point of rigor and severity, we believe to be quite unexampled in the annals of criticism." See Chalmers' Evidences, pp. 72-74.

52. See 1 Stark. on Ev. pp. 480, 545.

53. If the witnesses could be supposed to have been biased, this would not destroy their testimony to matters of fact; it would only detract from the weight of their judgment in matters of opinion. The rule of law on this subject has been thus stated by Dr. Lushington: "When you examine the testimony of wit-

nesses nearly connected with the parties, and there is nothing very peculiar tending to destroy their credit, when they depose to mere facts, their testimony is to be believed; when they depose as to matter of opinion, it is to be received with suspicion." Dillon *v.* Dillon, 3 Curteis's Eccl. Rep. pp. 96, 102.

54. This subject has been so fully treated by Dr. Paley, in his view of the Evidences of Christianity, Part I., Prop. I., that it is unnecessary to pursue it farther in this place.

55. 1 Stark. on Ev. pp. 483, 548.

56. Campbell's Philosophy of Rhetoric, c. v. b. 1. Part 3, p. 125; Whately's Rhetoric, part 1. ch. 2, § 4; 1 Stark. on Ev. p. 487.

57. See the Quarterly Review, vol. xxviii. p. 465. These narrators were, the Duchess D'Angouleme herself, the two Messrs. De Bouille, the Duc De Choiseul, his servant, James Brissac, Messrs. De Damas and Deslons, two of the officers commanding detachments on the road, Messrs. De Moustier and Valori, the garde du corps who accompanied the king, and finally M. de Fontanges, archbishop of Toulouse, who though not himself a party to the transaction, is supposed to have written from the information of the queen. An earlier instance of similar discrepancy is mentioned by Sully. After the battle of Aumale, in which Henry IV. was wounded, when the officers were around the king's bed, conversing upon the events of the day, there were not two who agreed in the recital of the most particular circumstance of the action. D'Aubigne, a contemporary writer, does not even mention the king's wound, though it was the only one he ever received in his life. See Memoirs of Sully, vol. i. p. 245. If we treated these narratives as sceptics would have us treat those of the sacred writers, what evidence should we have of any battle of Aumale, or of any flight to Varennes?

58. Far greater discrepancies can be found in the different reports of the same case, given by the reporters of legal judgments than are shown among the evangelists; and yet we do not consider them as detracting from the credit of the reporters, to whom

we still resort with confidence, as to good authority. Some of these discrepancies seem utterly irreconcilable. Thus, in a case, 45 Edw. III. 19, where the question was upon a gift of lands to J. de C. with Joan, the sister of the donor, and to their heirs, Fitzherbert (tit. *Tail*, 14) says it was adjudged a gift in frankmarriage; while Brook (tit. *Frankmarriage*) says it was not decided. Vid. 10 Co. 118. Others are irreconcilable, until the aid of a third reporter is invoked. Thus, in the case of Cooper *v.* Franklin, Croke says it was not decided, but adjourned (Cro. Jac. 100); Godbolt says it was decided in a certain way, which he mentions (Godb. 269); Moor also reports it as decided, but gives a different account of the question raised (Moor, 848); while Bulstrode gives a still different report of the judgment of the court, which he says was delivered by Croke himself. But by his account it further appears, that the case was previously twice argued; and thus it at length results that the other reporters relate only what fell from the court on each of the previous occasions. Other similar examples may be found in 1 Dougl. 6, n. compared with 5 East, 475, n. in the case of Galbraith *v.* Neville; and in that of Stoughton *v.* Reynolds, reported by Fortescue, Strange, and in Cases temp. Hardwicke. See 3 Barn. & A. 247, 248. Indeed, the books abound in such instances. Other discrepancies are found in the names of the same litigating parties, as differently given by reporters; such as Putt *v.* Roster, 2 Mod. 318; Foot *v.* Rastall, Skin. 49, and Putt *v.* Royston, 2 Show 211; also, Hosdell *v.* Harris. 2 Keb. 462; Hodson *v.* Harwich, Ib. 533, and Hodsden *v.* Harridge, 2 Saund. 64, and a multitude of others, which are universally admitted to mean the same cases, even when they are not precisely within the rule of *idem sonans.* These diversities, it is well known, have never detracted in the slightest degree from the estimation in which the reporters are all deservedly held, as authors of merit, enjoying to this day the confidence of the profession. Admitting now, for the sake of argument (what is not conceded in fact), that diversities equally great exist among the sacred writers, how can we consistently, and as lawyers, raise any serious objection against them on that account, or treat them in any manner different from that which we observe towards our reporters?

59. Mr. Hume's argument is thus refuted by Lord Brougham. "Here are two answers, to which the doctrine proposed by Mr. Hume is exposed, and either appears sufficient to shake it.

"*First*—Our belief in the uniformity of the laws of nature rests not altogether upon an experience. We believe no man ever was raised from the dead,—not merely because we ourselves never saw it, for indeed that would be a very limited ground of deduction; and our belief was fixed on the subject long before we had any considerable experience,—fixed chiefly by authority,—that is, by deference to other men's experience. We found our confident belief in this negative position partly, perhaps chiefly, upon the testimony of others; and at all events, our belief that in times before our own the same position held good, must of necessity be drawn from our trusting the relations of other men—that is, it depends upon the evidence of testimony. If, then, the existence of the law of nature is proved, in great part at least, by such evidence, can we wholly reject the like evidence when it comes to prove an exception to the rule—a deviation from the law? The more numerous are the cases of the law being kept—the more rare those of its being broken—the more scrupulous certainly ought we to be in admitting the proofs of the breach. But that testimony is capable of making good the proof there seems no doubt. In truth, the degree of excellence and of strength to which testimony may arise seems almost indefinite. There is hardly any cogency which it is not capable by possible supposition of attaining. The endless multiplication of witnesses,—the unbounded variety of their habits of thinking, their prejudices, their interests,—afford the means of conceiving the force of their testimony, augmented *ad infinitum*, because these circumstances afford the means of diminishing indefinitely the chances of their being all mistaken, all misled, or all combining to deceive us. Let any man try to calculate the chances of a thousand persons who come from different quarters, and never saw each other before, and who all vary in their habits, stations, opinions, interests,—being mistaken or combining to deceive us, when they give the same account of an event as having happened before their eyes,—these chances are many hundreds of thousands to one. And yet we can conceive them multiplied indefinitely; for one hundred thousand such witnesses may all in like manner bear the same testimony; and they may all tell us their story within twenty-four hours after the transaction, and in the next parish. And yet according to Mr. Hume's argument, we are bound to disbelieve them all, because they speak to a thing contrary to our own experience, and to the accounts which other witnesses had formerly given us of the laws of nature, and which our forefathers had handed down to us as derived from witnesses who lived in the old time before them. It is unnecessary to add that no testimony of the witnesses, whom we are supposing to concur in their relation, contradicts any testimony of our own senses. If it did, the argument would resemble Archbishop Tillotson's upon the Real Presence, and our disbelief would be at once warranted.

"*Secondly*—This leads us to the next objection to which Mr. Hume's argument is liable, and which we have in part anticipated while illustrating the first. He requires us to withhold our belief in circumstances which would force every man of common understanding to lend his assent, and to act upon the supposition of the story told being true. For, suppose either such numbers of various witnesses as we have spoken of; or, what is perhaps stronger, suppose a miracle reported to us, first by a number of relators, and then by three or four of the very soundest judges and most incorruptibly honest men we know,—men noted for their difficult belief of wonders, and, above all, steady unbelievers in miracles, without any bias in favor of religion, but rather accustomed to doubt, if not disbelieve,—most people would lend an easy belief to any miracle thus vouched. But let us add this circumstance, that a friend on his death-bed had been attended by us, and that we had told him a fact known only to ourselves, something that we had secretly done the very moment before we told it to the dying man, and which to no other being we had ever revealed,— and that the credible witnesses we are supposing, informed us that the deceased appeared to them, conversed with them, and remained with them a day or two, accompanying them, and to avouch the fact of his reappearance on this earth, communicated to them the secret of which we had made him the sole depositary the moment before his death;—according to Mr. Hume, we are bound rather to believe, not only that those credible witnesses deceived us, or that those sound and unprejudiced men were themselves deceived, and fancied things without real existence, but further, that they all hit by chance upon the discovery of a real secret, known only to ourselves and the dead man. Mr. Hume's argument requires us to believe this as the lesser improbability of the two—as less unlikely than the rising of one from the dead; and yet every one must feel convinced, that were he placed in the situation we have been figuring, he would not only lend his belief to the relation, but if the relators accompanied it with a special warning from the deceased person to avoid a certain contemplated act, he would, acting upon the belief of their story, take the warning, and avoid doing the forbidden deed. Mr. Hume's argument makes no exception. This is its scope; and whether he chooses to push it thus far or no, all miracles are of necessity denied by it, without the least regard to the kind or the quantity of the proof on which they are rested; and the testimony which we have supposed, accompanied by the test or check we have supposed, would fall within the grasp of the argument just as much and as clearly as any other miracle avouched by more ordinary combinations of evidence.

"The use of Mr. Hume's argument is this, and it is an important and a valuable one. It teaches us to sift closely and vigorously the evidence for miraculous events. It bids us remember that the probabilities are always, and must always be incomparably greater against, than for, the truth of these relations, because it is always far more likely that the testimony should be mistaken or false, than that the general laws of nature should be suspended. Further than this the doctrine cannot in soundness of reason be carried. It does not go the length of proving that those general laws cannot, by the force of human testimony, be shown to have been, in a particular instance, and with a particular purpose, suspended." See his Discourse of Natural Theology. Note 5, p. 210-214, ed. 1835.

Laplace, in his Essai sur les Probabilités, maintains that, the more extraordinary the fact attested, the greater the probability of error or falsehood in the attestor. Simple good sense, he says, suggests this; and the calculation of probabilities confirms its suggestion. There are some things, he adds, so extraordinary, that nothing can balance their improbability. The position here laid down is, that the probability of error, or of the falsehood of testimony, becomes *in proportion* greater, as the fact which is attested is more extraordinary. And hence a fact extraordinary in the highest possible degree, becomes in the highest possible degree improbable; or so much so, that nothing can counterbalance its improbability.

This argument has been made much use of, to discredit the evidence of miracles, and the truth of that divine religion which is attested by them. But however sound it may be, in one sense, this application of it is fallacious. The fallacy lies in the meaning affixed to the term "extraordinary." If Laplace means a fact extraordinary *under* its existing circumstances and relations, that is, a fact remaining extraordinary, notwithstanding all its circumstances, the position needs not here to be controverted. But if the term means extraordinary *in the abstract*, it is far from being universally true, or affording a correct test of truth, or rule of evidence. Thus, it is extraordinary that a man should leap fifteen feet at a bound; but not extraordinary that a strong and active man should do it, under a sudden impulse to save his life. The former is improbable in the abstract; the latter is rendered probable by the circumstances. So, things extraordinary, and therefore improbable under one hypothesis, become the reverse under another. Thus, the occurrence of a violent storm at sea, and the utterance by Jesus of the words, "Peace, be still," succeeded instantly by a perfect calm, are facts which, taken separately from each other, are not in themselves extraordinary. The connection between the command of Jesus and the ensuing calm, as cause and effect, would be extraordinary and improbable if he were a mere man; but it becomes perfectly natural and probable, when his divine power is considered. Each of those facts is in its nature so simple and obvious, that the most ignorant person is capable of observing it. There is nothing extraordinary in the facts themselves; and the extraordinary coincidence, in which the miracle consists, becomes both intelligible and probable upon the hypothesis of the Christian. See the *Christian Observer* for Oct. 1838, p. 617. The theory of Laplace may, with the same propriety, be applied to the creation of the world. That matter was created out of nothing is extremely improbable, in the abstract, that is, if there is no God; and therefore it is not to be believed. But if the existence of a Supreme Being is conceded, the fact is perfectly credible.

Laplace was so fascinated with his theory, that he thought the calculus of probabilities might be usefully employed in discovering the value of the different methods resorted to, in those sciences which are in a great measure conjectural, as medicine, agriculture, and political economy. And he proposed that there should be kept, in every branch of the administration, an exact register of the trials made of different measures, and of the results, whether good or bad, to which they have led. See the *Edinburgh Review*, vol. xxiii. pp. 335, 336. Napoleon, who appointed him Minister of the Interior, has thus described him: "A geometrician of the first class, he did not reach mediocrity as a statesman. He never viewed any subject in its true light; he was always occupied with subtleties; his notions were all problematic; and he carried into the administration the spirit of the *infinitely small*." See the *Encyclopaedia Britannica*, art. Laplace, vol. xiii. p. 101; Memoires Ecrits â Ste. Helena, i. 3. The injurious effect of deductive reasoning, upon the minds of those who addict themselves to this method alone, to the exclusion of all other modes of arriving at the knowledge of truth in fact, is shown with great clearness and success, by Mr. Whewel, in the ninth of the Bridgwater Treatises, book 3, ch. 6. The calculus of probabilities has been applied by some writers to judicial evidence; but its very slight value as a test, is clearly shown in an able article on Presumptive Evidence, in the *Law Magazine*, vol. 1. pp. 28-32 (New Series).

60. See Mr. Norton's "Discourse on the latest form of Infidelity," p. 18.

61. The arguments on this subject are stated in a condensed form, by Mr. Horne, in his Introduction to the Study of the Holy Scriptures, vol i. ch. 4, sec. 2; in which he refers, among others, to Dr. Gregory's Letters on the Evidences of the Christian Revelation; Dr. Campbell's Dissertation on Miracles; Vince's Sermons on the Credibility of Miracles; Bishop Marsh's Lectures, part 6, lect. 30; Dr. Adams's Treatise in reply to Mr. Heum; Bishop Gleig's Dissertation on Miracles, (in the third volume of his edition of Stackhouse's History of the Bible, p. 240, &c.); Dr. Key's Norissian Lectures, vol. i. See also Dr. Howell's Lowell Lectures, lect. I. and II, delivered in Boston in 1844, where the topic is treated with great perspicuity and cogency.

Among the more popular treaties on miracles, are Bogue's Essay on the Divine Authority of the New Testament, ch. 5; Bishop Wilson's Evidences of Christianity, vol. 1. lect. 7; Bishop Sumner's Evidences, ch. 10; Gambier's Guide to the Study of Moral Evidence, ch. 5; Mr. Norton's Discourse on the latest form of Infidelity, and Dr. Dewey's Dudleian Lecture, delivered before Harvard University, in May, 1836.

62. See Bishop Wilson's Evidences, lect. 7, p. 130.

63. 1 Stark. on Ev. p. 496-499.

64. 1 Stark. on Ev. p. 523.

65. 1 Stark. on Ev. p. 487. The Gospels abound in instances of this. See, for example, Mark, xv. 21; John, xviii. 10; Luke, xxiii. 6; Matt. xxvii 58-60; John xi. 1.

66. 1 Stark. on Ev. pp. 522, 585.

67. See 1 Stark. oñ Ev. p. 498. Willis on Circumstantial Evidence, pp. 128, 129.

68. See Chalmers' Evidence, chap. iii.

69. See Chalmers' Evidence, pp. 76-78, Amer. ed. Proofs of this kind are copiously referred to by Mr. Horne, in his Introduction, &c. vol. i., ch. 3, sect. II. 2.

70. See Mark viii. 32; ix. 5; and xiv. 29; Matt. xvi. 22; and xvii. 5; Luke ix. 33; and xviii. 18; John xiii. 8; and xviii. 15.

71. Mark viii. 29; Matt. xvi. 16; Luke ix. 20.

72. Matt. xviii. 21; and xix. 27; John xiii. 36.

73. Gal. ii. 11.

74. John xx. 3-6.

75. Matt. xiv. 30.

76. Acts i. 15.

77. Acts ii. 14.

78. Matt. xvi. 16; Mark viii. 29; Luke ix. 20; John vi. 69.

79. Matt. xxvi. 33, 35; Mark xiv. 29.

80. See Paley's view of the Evidences of Christianity, part ii. chapters iii. iv. v. vi. vii.; Ib. part iii. ch. i.; Chalmers on the Evidence and Authority of the Christian Revelation, ch. iii. iv. viii.; Wilson's Evidences of Christianity, lect. vi.; Bogue's Essay on the Divine Authority of the New Testament, chap. iii. iv.

81. See Bogue's Essay, ch. i. sec. 2; Newcome's Obs. part ii. ch. i. sec. 14.

Index of Names

Index of Cases Cited

Works by John Warwick Montgomery

The Altizer-Montgomery Dialogue (with Thomas J.J. Altizer)
Christianity for the Tough-Minded
*Chytraeus on Sacrifice: A Reformation Treatise in Biblical
    Theology*
¿Como sabemos que hay un Dios? (in Spanish)
Computers, Cultural Change, and the Christ (trilingual:
    English, French, German)
Crisis in Lutheran Theology
Cross and Crucible (2 volumes)
Damned Through the Church
*Demon Possession**
Ecumenicity, Evangelicals, and Rome
¿Es Confiable el Cristianismo? (in Spanish)
Evidence for Faith: Deciding the God Question
*God's Inerrant Word**
History and Christianity
How Do We Know There Is a God?
Human Rights and Human Dignity
In Defense of Martin Luther
*International Scholars Directory**
The 'Is God Dead?' Controversy
*Jurisprudence: A Book of Readings**
La Mort de Dieu (in French)
The Law Above the Law
The Marxist Approach to Human Rights: Analysis and Critique
*Myth, Allegory and Gospel**
Principalities and Powers: The World of the Occult, 2nd ed.
The Quest for Noah's Ark, 2nd ed.
*A Seventeenth-Century View of European Libraries**
The Shape of the Past
The Shaping of America
Situation Ethics: True or False? (with Joseph Fletcher)
The Suicide of Christian Theology
*The Union List of Serial Publications in Chicago-Area
    Protestant Theological Libraries**
Verdammt durch die Kirche? (in German)
Where Is History Going?
Wohin Marschiert China? (in German)
The Writing of Research Papers in Theology

---

*Works edited by Dr. Montgomery